WELCOMING

KITCHEN

WELCOMING

KITCHEN

200

DELICIOUS ALLERGEN- & GLUTEN-FREE VEGAN RECIPES

KIM LUTZ

with MEGAN HART, MS, RD

STERLING
New York

STERLING
New York

An Imprint of Sterling Publishing
387 Park Avenue South
New York, NY 10016

ISBN 978-1-4027-7185-9 (hardcover)
ISBN 978-1-4027-8899-4 (ebook)

Distributed in Canada by Sterling Publishing
c/o Canadian Manda Group, 165 Dufferin Street
Toronto, Ontario, Canada M6K 3H6
Distributed in the United Kingdom by GMC Distribution Services
Castle Place, 166 High Street, Lewes, East Sussex, England BN7 1XU
Distributed in Australia by Capricorn Link (Australia) Pty. Ltd.
P.O. Box 704, Windsor, NSW 2756, Australia

A Buoy Point Media Production
Interior Design: Fabia Wargin

For information about custom editions, special sales, and premium
and corporate purchases, please contact Sterling Special Sales
at 800-805-5489 or specialsales@sterlingpublishing.com.

Manufactured in the United States of America

2 4 6 8 10 9 7 5 3 1

www.sterlingpublishing.com

DEDICATION

....

For my boys,
Casey, Evan, and Steve

....

ACKNOWLEDGMENTS

· ·

This has been a long labor of love. I have been working on this book for close to five years. Lucky for me, I've had great support every step of the way.

Three women have stood by my side to make this book a reality. Megan Hart has written with me, listened to me, answered endless e-mails, and provided essential guidance. This book is immeasurably better because of her contributions. My agent, Gina Panettieri, not only believed in my project, but provided great feedback so that it could have a chance to find a publishing home. Once we found that home at Sterling, Jennifer Williams taught me how to turn recipes into a cook-book. She helped me to find my voice in the midst of teaspoons and mixing bowls.

A huge thank you goes to Fabia Wargin for creating such a fabulous design for my book; and to Lary Rosenblatt and Laurie Lieb at Buoy Point Media Production for pulling it all together.

I owe a huge debt of gratitude to my loving family and friends. My sons, Casey and Evan, provided the inspiration to take on this challenge; they are the best assistants any mom could have. My husband, Steve, was my rock during this process. He put up with a lot of mess, a lot of single-minded focus, and a lot of calories. I am so glad to have him in my corner. My parents (all of them) gave me the belief that I could do anything, especially my mom, who taught me how to cook. My sister, Laura, has stood side by side with me through every adventure I've taken, including this one. The sister of my heart, Dana Kissinger, cheered me along the way, and Mark Collantes has been a true friend. I have had an awesome crew of tastetesters. Rob and Matthew Sagami and Paige Miller have tasted the vast majority of these recipes, whether they were hungry or not! I started on this project because Joelle Gary gave me the idea and Rob Sagami helped bring it to life.

In addition to old friends, I am grateful to the support that I've received from new friends in the gluten-free and allergen-free communities.

CONTENTS

MY STORY

Eight years ago, I gave birth to a beautiful baby boy. Within a couple of months, he was covered in bloody scabs and had developed breathing problems. Over the next few months, we learned that he had many food allergies (cows' milk, eggs, and tree nuts). Because I was breast-feeding, I had to eliminate these foods from my diet. Going to the grocery store after learning about Casey's food restrictions was devastating. I stood in the aisles and cried because it seemed as though there was nothing I could buy. Even though Casey was just a baby, my husband and I considered what a life without birthday cake and Halloween treats would be like. That just wasn't an option for us, so I set out to learn how to cook for my baby. Along the way, we realized that many people around us were also living with food restrictions. We wanted our home to be a welcoming place, where everyone could sit around the table together and enjoy great meals.

. . . .

The results of the recipes in this book are delicious dishes that can be enjoyed by everyone, whether you have food restrictions or not. Now, from birthday parties and play dates to holiday dinners and game-day buffets, you can serve delicious food that satisfies every guest. I hope these recipes transform your home into a welcoming kitchen.

A WELCOMING KITCHEN

These days, creating a welcoming kitchen—a place where friends and family come together to enjoy each other's company and great food—can be a challenge in light of increasing rates of food allergies, sensitivities, and restrictions. This book will help you bring the joy back into your cooking by providing you with tasty recipes that are free of eight of the most common food allergens—peanuts, tree nuts, eggs, dairy, soy, wheat, fish, and shellfish. You will not find any sesame— a potentially life-threatening allergen—in the recipes, either, and all recipes are vegan and gluten-free. In the welcoming kitchen, everyone can sit down and eat together; no one needs to feel left out.

By using varied ingredients, *Welcoming Kitchen* recipes bring diversity to a diet without restrictions. For example, many vegans over-rely on the ease of using soy and wheat in meal preparation. Since these recipes don't include either, they can provide a way to deliciously incorporate other grains and protein sources without a struggle.

My philosophy can best be described as lowest-common-denominator cooking in the sense that it is safe for just about everyone. Every recipe in this book fits the allergy-free, gluten-free, and vegan model. Even better, each has been tested by a wide variety of eaters, from carnivores and bread lovers to processed-food junkies and health-food fans, and every recipe has passed the most important test—the taste test. With the recipes in this book you can substitute ingredients that are safe for the crowd you're feeding and they'll still come out just right every time. For example, if you're making blueberry muffins and don't need them to be gluten-free, you can substitute all-purpose flour or "regular" oat flour. If soy is not an issue, you can use soy milk instead of rice milk.

This "welcoming" approach to cooking can find a place in every cook's repertoire. Need a delicious salad to bring to a potluck dinner or a safe snack for kids on a play date? No problem. You've got it covered. With the recipes in this book you can cook delicious meals for any occasion that are appropriate for a variety of diets and guests, whether they're vegans, lactose-intolerant, or allergic to nuts, and everyone will have a great time.

This book can help you transform your kitchen into a welcoming kitchen only if you can easily prepare the dishes. With that in mind, I've tried to keep things as uncomplicated as possible. Sometimes this means using canned or frozen produce (you can always substitute fresh ingredients) or eliminating extra steps. I've also tried to keep the ingredients accessible. I know that not everyone lives in an area where there are lots of high-end grocery stores, so I've tried to keep to basic ingredients whenever possible. In the section on the *Welcoming Kitchen* Pantry (page 4), I provide further explanation.

BASICS

....

These recipes were created to make it easy and affordable to feed all of your guests, even those with restricted diets. Since you don't need to use exotic ingredients it's easy to whip up a meal or snack, whether you're serving folks with special diet needs on a daily basis or just occasionally. In fact, you can find most of the ingredients for these recipes in any well-stocked grocery store or from online vendors. Before you get started, here are a few tips to make things a little easier—and a little safer.

Communication Is the First Ingredient

Make sure that you talk to your doctor or dietitian about which foods are safe for you and which should be avoided. Ask for a list of ingredients you should avoid and bring this information with you when you shop. Remember that ingredients in prepared foods can change, so always check the ingredient label: even a tried-and-true favorite might be unsafe after the manufacturer changes the recipe. If you are preparing food for others, you also need to communicate with your guests to learn what steps you should take to ensure a safe dining experience for all. Once you know which ingredients you can use, you can get cooking!

Experimenting with Substitutes

Don't expect these recipes to have the same taste and texture as your Aunt Betty's. Enjoy them for the unique creations that they are, rather than trying to replicate a well-loved dish. You just might discover some new favorites.

As in all cooking, using the best and freshest ingredients you can find will yield the best-tasting results. Feel free to experiment. For example, if a recipe calls for broccoli and the farmers' market has beautiful, fresh asparagus, give it a try instead. No recipe is completely graven in stone. Part of the joy of a welcoming kitchen is having fun while you're cooking.

It is crucial for you to become informed about hidden sources of must-avoid ingredients. There are very thorough lists available through your doctor or on the Internet for every possible dietary restriction. Knowledge is power. Here are some examples:

- Some canola and olive oil sprays contain lecithin, which is derived from soy or eggs. To ensure that your oil spray contains *just oil,* fill a manual-pump spray can with your choice of oil.

- Vanilla extract can be a source of gluten, so seek out vanillas that are labeled gluten-free if you are baking without gluten.

- Wine and beer can be hidden sources of eggs, milk, or fish, since beverage makers sometimes use these ingredients in the filtering (or fining) process. Seek out vegan wine or beer instead.

- If you need to avoid dairy products, you can use yogurt made from coconut milk to add extra creaminess to both sweet and savory dishes. If your local natural-foods store doesn't carry coconut-based yogurt (the So Delicious brand produces a range of flavors), you can ask the grocer to order a case for you. If you're not going to use all the yogurt before the expiration date, you can freeze, thaw, and cook with it later on.

No Fancy Gadgets Required

You will not need any fancy kitchen equipment to pull off the recipes in this book. A blender and a food processor make life easier, but you can get by without them, and although an immersion blender can make cooking soups a lot quicker and neater (not to mention more fun), it's not essential. In fact, I didn't get one of these for myself until after I'd developed all the recipes in this book!

The Welcoming Kitchen Pantry

If you're not cooking with wheat or dairy, eggs or soy, what can you use? That's a good question! You can make hearty stews and soups using a wide range of vegetables and beans, and enjoy dozens of delicious casseroles, risottos, and pastas. You can even make scrumptious brownies, cakes, and cookies! You just need to have the right ingredients and a few tips to create safe, delicious dishes that will delight your guests.

Whenever possible, I have tried to use ingredients that won't be too hard to find. Most of the ingredients mentioned in *Welcoming Kitchen* can be purchased at a well-stocked supermarket. Others (such as coconut-milk yogurt or nutritional yeast) might require a trip to your local health or natural-foods store. There are also helpful resources available on the Internet that can make finding allergy-specific ingredients a whole lot easier.

So...you want to get started. First, you have to go shopping. What should you buy to turn *Welcoming Kitchen* recipes into delicious dishes? Take a look at these exciting ingredients:

Fresh fruits and vegetables.
Fresh, in-season, organic produce is best. Frozen fruit can be helpful to keep on hand for smoothies and muffins in the winter, and some basic canned and frozen vegetables, like pumpkin, tomatoes, and spinach, mean that it's always possible to pull off a fresh-tasting dinner.

Pumpkin seeds (pepitas) and sunflower seeds.
Always be sure to check the label on the packaging to make sure these seeds are not contaminated with nuts (if you need them to be nut-free). Halloween jack-o'-lanterns are a great source of safe pepitas, even if removing the pumpkin seeds from their shells is somewhat time-consuming. You can

then freeze and use the shelled pepitas over the next six months. If you're going to use them right away, dry pepitas stored in a jar will stay fresh in your refrigerator for a few weeks. You can also plant a few sunflowers in your yard for a safe source of delicious seeds (not to mention a beautiful backyard).

Sunflower seed butter. Although it is available commercially, sunflower seed butter can be contaminated with soy, so if you need it to be soy-free, you can make your own with sunflower seeds that are safe.

All-fruit preserves. All-fruit blends keep extra sugar out of your finished dishes.

Raisins, dried cranberries, and cherries. Check the package to ensure that these fruits are free of other allergens (i.e., they haven't been in contact with equipment that also processes nuts).

Pure maple syrup. Grade B will work equally well in these recipes as Grade A. Just be sure that it's pure maple syrup and not pancake syrup, which may be nothing more than colored high-fructose corn syrup and a bunch of other additives.

Applesauce. Baking in this book relies heavily on applesauce and baking powder to take the place of eggs in traditional recipes. Whether you're buying applesauce in a jar or making your own and freezing or canning it in batches, it's best to use organic fruit. Apples frequently top lists of produce that contain the highest pesticide loads. (The Environmental Working Group publishes a list of produce that should always be bought organic. Take a look at *www.foodnews.org*.)

Apple juice. Use 100% apple juice, not a juice-flavored drink that's mostly sugar with some apple flavor thrown in. Again, you should look for organic.

Coconut. Although the Food and Drug Administration (FDA) lists coconut as a tree nut, for purposes of allergy food labeling, many experts, including the Food Allergy and Anaphylaxis Network, do not consider coconut a tree nut. I use coconut as an ingredient in this book. Although allergy to coconut is rare, you should check with your doctor if you have any concerns.

Coconut milk. It's a good idea to keep extra cans of coconut milk, either light or regular, on hand to use as a replacement for rice milk if you run out or as a quick whipped topping alternative.

Coconut-milk yogurts. These come in a variety of flavors. If your food store doesn't stock them, ask your grocer to order a case and then freeze what you're not going to use right away. Thawed yogurts will still work well in recipes because the taste remains the same, although the texture may change a little after thawing. If you or your guests are allergic to coconut, use a rice-based yogurt instead.

Rice milk. Use rice milk that is fortified with calcium and vitamins D and B12 if you need to get more of these in your diet.

Canned or dried beans (garbanzo, black beans, pinto beans, etc.). Dried beans are more economical than canned, but for throwing a quick dish together, canned beans cannot be beat for convenience.

Chipotle peppers in adobo sauce. You can find these versatile peppers in the ethnic food aisle of your grocery store.

Vegan bouillon and/or vegetable broth. While it's best to make your own vegetable broth and freeze it for future use, it's not always possible. No worries: boxed broth and bouillon cubes are a convenient way to add a dash of flavor. Just double check to make sure they're gluten-free (if that's one of your food requirements). If you have broth on hand and a recipe calls for bouillon, simply omit the water and bouillon and use the broth instead. You might need to add a little extra salt.

Rice. Arborio, short-grain brown, long-grain brown, organic basmati—there are many great options. Store rice in the refrigerator to extend its shelf life.

Oats. While almost all commercially available oats are contaminated with a gluten-containing grain (wheat, barley, or rye), certified gluten-free oats and oat flour are available and make good substitutes. Most people with celiac disease are able to tolerate some quantity of gluten-free oats, so it's worth checking with your doctor to see if you can incorporate this whole grain into your diet, even if you have to avoid gluten.

Cornmeal. Cornmeal can step in for bread crumbs in a lot of traditional recipes that require breading. For folks who can't eat corn due to an allergy, you can do the substitution backward—try gluten-free bread crumbs in place of cornmeal in some recipes (for example, see Italian Eggplant on page 94).

Kasha. Although kasha can refer to a number of grains, in these recipes I prefer to use roasted buckwheat.

Quinoa. This high-protein grain is becoming increasingly available, and you should be able to find it in large grocery stores. If your store doesn't stock it, you can order it online.

Gluten-free all-purpose baking flour. There is a wide range of brands with different "flour" combinations. Experiment to find the one you like best. If you're using a flour combo that includes a binding agent—either guar gum or xanthan gum—omit xanthan gum in the recipe.

Xanthan gum. Since gluten is the protein that holds traditional baked goods together, you need to use a binder when using gluten-free flours (except oat flour). Xanthan gum will take the place of the gluten in your gluten-free baking.

Cocoa. Since a lot of cocoa companies also make chocolate products that contain either nuts or milk, you should check with the company to be sure that your cocoa is uncontaminated with these ingredients.

Allergen-free chocolate chips. These chocolate chips are free of dairy, nuts, soy, and gluten.

Sugar. Recipes in this book call for a variety of sweeteners, including granulated sugar (I use vegan, evaporated cane juice), brown sugar, agave nectar, and maple syrup. If you avoid refined sugar, you can substitute agave nectar or fruit juice concentrate. Just remember that if you are substituting a liquid sweetener for a dry sweetener, you will need to reduce the other liquids in the recipe.

Nutritional yeast. Nutritional yeast is not the same as baker's yeast, which is not safe to eat on its own. Nutritional yeast can be added to dairy-free cooking to add dimension and a pleasant, cheesy flavor.

APPETIZERS & SNACKS

. . . .

What's a party without hors d'oeuvres? What's a play date without snacks? Just not as enjoyable, if you ask me! Whether you're throwing an elegant cocktail party or feeding a bunch of kids after school, you need to have go-to recipes that you know will please even the pickiest eater. So go ahead and worry about what color napkins to use, but with these recipes, you won't need to worry about what to serve your guests (even if they have restricted diets).

Sunflower Seed Butter

Ever since I started using sunflower seed butter as a substitute for peanut butter, friends and relatives have become fans of this yummy spread. Commercial sunflower seed butters are available in jars, but some are made in facilities that also process soy or nuts, so if you're concerned about allergen contamination, you can always make your own. Use sunflower seed butter as a 1 to 1 replacement in recipes that call for peanut butter. Also spread it on toast for sandwiches, blend it into a smoothie, or use it to fill celery stalks for a crunchy snack.

Makes about ¼ cup

½ cup roasted sunflower seeds

1 tbsp canola oil

Grind sunflower seeds in a food processor. Slowly drizzle in oil, ½ teaspoon at a time, until smooth.

Store sunflower seed butter in a sealed jar in the refrigerator. It will keep for about a week.

Per 1 tbsp serving: 124 calories, 11 g fat, 4 g carbohydrates, 1 g fiber, 3 g protein

Pumpkin Seed Butter

Pumpkin seed butter steps in when you need a substitute for peanut butter but can't eat sunflower seeds. The amount of oil that you should use depends on the desired consistency; more oil will result in a thinner pumpkin seed butter.

Makes about ½ cup

1 cup shelled pumpkin seeds (pepitas)

1 tbsp canola oil

   salt (optional)

Preheat oven to 200°F.

Spread pumpkin seeds on an ungreased cookie sheet. Bake for 10 minutes.

Grind warm pumpkin seeds in food processor. Once the pumpkin seeds are completely ground, slowly add a thin stream of canola oil until butter is the desired consistency. Add salt to taste.

Keep pumpkin seed butter in a sealed container in the refrigerator. It will keep for about a week.

Per 1 tbsp serving: 82 calories, 7 g fat, 2 g carbohydrates, 1 g fiber, 5 g protein

Yogurt Cheese Spread

Coconut-based yogurt is a great alternative to cream cheese. (You can also use rice-based yogurt.) Experiment with different flavors. Vanilla, for example, makes a great spread for Zucchini Bread (page 158), while plain yogurt works better for cooking.

Makes ½ cup

1   *6-ounce container vanilla-flavored coconut-based yogurt*

Place a fine-mesh colander or strainer in a bowl with enough room to keep yogurt out of excess water that will collect at the bottom of the bowl. Line strainer with a coffee filter. Scoop yogurt into the filter.

Cover and refrigerate for 6 hours or overnight. Scoop out yogurt "cheese" and keep in a lidded jar.

Per ½ cup serving: 87 calories, 4 g fat, 9 g carbohydrates, 2 g fiber, 1 g protein

A SPREAD OF SPREADS

Top crostini with any of the spreads that follow (Bruschetta, Mixed Mushroom Sauté, Olivada, or Roasted Fennel Spread) for an elegant appetizer, or toss the spread with pasta for an interesting entrée.

Crostini

Makes 4 pieces

2   slices gluten-free bread (for example, tapioca, brown rice, or white rice)

1   garlic clove

Toast both pieces of bread until light brown.

Cut garlic clove in half. Rub garlic on warm toast. Cut toast in half. (It looks nice cut on the diagonal.)

Per piece: 38 calories, 2 g fat, 5 g carbohydrates, 0 g fiber, 1 g protein

Bruschetta

If you need to throw together an appetizer in a pinch and you don't
have ripe tomatoes on hand, you can substitute drained, diced,
canned tomatoes.

Makes 2½ cups

2	tomatoes
¼	cup sliced basil leaves
½	cup rinsed and drained cannellini beans
¼	tsp salt
	freshly ground pepper to taste

Cut tomatoes in half. Gently squeeze
tomatoes to remove seeds; scoop out
remaining seeds with your finger or a
spoon. Chop tomatoes into half-inch pieces.

Toss tomatoes, sliced basil leaves, and
beans with salt and pepper.

Let sit for at least an hour to allow
flavors to blend.

Per ½ cup serving: 35 calories, 0 g fat, 7 g carbohydrates, 3 g fiber, 2 g protein

Mixed Mushroom Sauté

I feature mushrooms on the menu when I'm feeding a particularly carnivorous crowd. Their earthy texture pleases everyone!

Makes 1½ cups

1	tbsp olive oil
2	shallots, minced
1½	tbsps fresh rosemary, chopped
1	pound mixed mushrooms (oyster, cremini, shiitake, etc.)
¼	cup vegan red wine
⅛	tsp salt
	freshly ground pepper

Heat olive oil over medium heat in a medium skillet. Add shallots and rosemary, and heat 1 to 2 minutes.

Add mushrooms and sauté until tender.

Add wine, salt, and pepper. Cook until liquid is reduced.

Per ¼ cup serving: 60 calories, 2 g fat, 4 g carbohydrates, 1 g fiber, 2 g protein

Olivada

I love olives! This spread is the perfect combination of salty and flavorful.

Makes 1 cup

4	*sun-dried tomato halves*
1	*garlic clove*
1	*tbsp olive oil*
½	*cup pitted green olives*
½	*cup pitted kalamata olives*
1	*tsp capers*

Cover sun-dried tomatoes with boiling water. Set aside for 5 minutes.

Smash garlic clove with the side of a large knife. In a small bowl or coffee cup, combine olive oil and garlic clove. Heat oil and garlic in microwave oven on high for 20 seconds. (Or you can heat oil and garlic in a small saucepan over medium heat for a minute or two—until garlic becomes fragrant.) Remove garlic clove from oil.

Remove sun-dried tomatoes from water. Combine softened tomatoes, flavored oil, olives, and capers in food processor. Pulse until the mixture becomes a rough paste.

Per 2 tbsp serving: 36 calories, 4 g fat, 1 g carbohydrates, 1 g fiber, 0 g protein

Roasted Fennel Spread

We take part in a Community Supported Agriculture (CSA) farm, where we get a box of seasonal produce every week. Whenever fennel shows up in my CSA produce basket, I whip up a batch of this spread. It makes even a Tuesday feel special, particularly when tossed with pasta for a quick, but lovely, dinner.

Makes 1½ cups

1	fennel bulb
2	medium zucchini
3–4	garlic cloves
1	pint cherry tomatoes
2	tbsps olive oil
	salt & pepper to taste
½	cup vegan red wine

Preheat oven to 425.

Cut away tough end and leafy green top of fennel bulb. Slice fennel bulb in ¼- to ½-inch-thick slices.

Slice zucchini into thick slices (1½ to 2 inches).

On a cookie sheet or jelly roll pan, toss all vegetables with the olive oil, salt, and pepper.

Roast 15 to 20 minutes, or until vegetables are soft and starting to brown.

Puree all vegetables in a food processor until smooth.

In a small saucepan, combine vegetable puree with wine. Bring to a high simmer to burn off alcohol.

Per 1 tbsp serving: 21 calories, 1 g fat, 2 g carbohydrates, 1 g fiber, 0 g protein

Chipotle Guacamole

This guacamole has a nice kick and a bright fresh look. Unless you cover it carefully, though, oxygen will start to discolor the top layer after just a few minutes. To avoid this, press a piece of plastic wrap right onto the surface of the guacamole and refrigerate. Uncover just before serving.

Makes 4 servings

2	*medium avocados*
½	*medium onion*
1	*medium tomato*
1–2	*canned chipotle peppers in adobo sauce (depending on desired heat)*
2	*tbsps cilantro*
1	*tbsp lime juice*

Mash avocados with potato masher or fork.

Medium chop onion and tomatoes.

Take peppers out of sauce.

Finely chop peppers and cilantro.

Mix all ingredients.

Per serving: 191 calories, 15 g fat, 16 g carbohydrates, 9 g fiber, 7 g protein

Polenta and Herb-Stuffed Mushrooms

Served with a beautiful green salad and fresh fruit, these stuffed mushrooms make an elegant lunch entrée.

Makes 24 mushrooms (6 servings)

24	medium white mushrooms
⅜	cup coarse cornmeal
1¼	cups water, divided
3	tbsps olive oil, divided
2	garlic cloves, minced
1	small onion, minced
3	tbsps vegan white wine
¼	tsp dried thyme
⅛	tsp poultry seasoning
⅛	tsp salt
¼	tsp black pepper

Preheat the oven to 350°F.

Clean mushrooms with a damp cloth or a stiff vegetable brush. Remove and mince the stems; set aside mushroom caps and stems.

In a small bowl, mix cornmeal with ¼ cup water. In a medium saucepan, bring 1 cup water to a boil. Lower heat to medium and slowly whisk in cornmeal mixture. Continue stirring until cornmeal mixture (polenta) thickens and begins to pull away from the sides of the pot.

Heat 1 tablespoon olive oil over medium flame. Add garlic, onion, and minced mushroom stems. Sauté until golden. Add wine, thyme, poultry seasoning, salt, and pepper. Add polenta; stir to combine.

Oil a shallow baking dish with 1 tablespoon olive oil. Stuff the mushroom caps with the polenta mixture. Sprinkle the mushrooms with the remaining tablespoon of olive oil.

Bake 45 minutes.

Per serving: 134 calories, 8 g fat, 13 g carbohydrates, 2 g fiber, 3 g protein

Creamy Dill Dip

The creamy goodness of this dilly of a dip works just as well as a salad dressing or topping for baked potatoes as it does for fresh veggies and chips. Yum.

Makes 1½ cups

2   6-ounce containers of plain coconut-based yogurt

2   tbsps finely chopped fresh dill

2   cloves minced garlic

¾   tsp seasoned salt

In a small bowl, mix all ingredients.

Chill before serving.

Per ¼ cup serving: 44 calories, 2 g fat, 5 g carbohydrates, 1 g fiber, 0 g protein

Pesto-Stuffed Cherry Tomatoes

To make these little tomatoes stand upright (and look great on the plate), slice a thin layer off the bottom of each tomato.

Makes 6 servings (4 tomatoes per serving)

¼ cup Basil Pesto
(page 114)

24 cherry tomatoes

Thoroughly wash cherry tomatoes. Remove stems and core each tomato. Remove seeds with a small spoon or your finger.

Fill the center of each tomato with pesto.

Per serving: 33 calories, 2 g fat, 3 g carbohydrates, 1 g fiber, 2 g protein

Artichoke Fritters

My husband, Steve, my sister, Laura, and I all love these crunchy-tender delights. They make a great starter to an Italian-themed dinner party.

Makes approximately 16 fritters

1	15-ounce can artichoke hearts
1	cup cornmeal
1½	tsps garlic pepper
⅛–¼	tsp cayenne (optional)
½	cup rice milk
	canola oil

Drain and thoroughly rinse artichoke hearts, and then drain again. Slice artichoke hearts in half.

In a shallow bowl, combine cornmeal, garlic pepper, and cayenne if using.

Pour rice milk into another bowl.

Heat oil in a medium skillet until shimmery.

Dip artichokes, one at a time, into the rice milk, then into the cornmeal mixture. Use a spoon to ensure that all of the artichoke is covered.

Fry the artichokes until golden on one side, and then turn to cook on the other side. Place cooked artichokes onto a paper-towel-lined plate to drain.

Per fritter: 95 calories, 6 g fat, 11 g carbohydrates, 0.5 g fiber, 1 g protein

Sesame-Free Hummus

This creamy hummus has a lemony zing. Although traditional hummus recipes call for tahini, a paste made from sesame seeds, I've left it out of this recipe to keep it safe for anyone who has a sesame allergy. Hummus is a staple in my son Casey's lunch box. He loves hummus and avocado sandwiches, and his younger brother Evan likes to dip tortilla chips in hummus. We usually store hummus in a jar and scoop it out for sandwiches, but if you want a fancier presentation, spread it on a plate and top with olive oil and paprika. For a thinner spread, you can add vegetable broth or more olive oil, one teaspoon at a time, until it reaches the consistency you desire.

Makes 6 servings

1   15-ounce can garbanzo beans, drained and rinsed

2   tbsps lemon juice (fresh is best, but bottled will work)

3   tbsps olive oil

1   clove of garlic

¼   tsp cumin

¼   tsp salt

Combine all ingredients in a food processor or blender. Blend until smooth.

Per serving: 145 calories, 8 g fat, 16 g carbohydrate, 3 g fiber, 4 g protein

Italian Hummus

This Italian take on a bean dip or bean spread incorporates basil, garlic, and sun-dried tomato into a cannellini bean mash.

Makes 6 servings

4	*sun-dried tomato halves*
1	*15-ounce can cannellini beans (white kidney beans)*
2	*tbsps fresh basil, sliced*
3	*garlic cloves, minced*
3	*tbsps olive oil*
2	*tbsps lemon juice*
¼	*tsp white pepper*

Soak sun-dried tomatoes in boiling water for 10 minutes.

Drain and rinse cannellini beans.

Combine all ingredients in a food processor. Blend until smooth.

Per serving: 166 calories, 7 g fat, 21 g carbohydrates, 5 g fiber, 6 g protein

Lime-Lover's Salsa

Not only does this salsa make a great dip, it's a terrific salad dressing, too.

Makes 1½ cups

4	roma (plum) tomatoes	Slice tomatoes in half and remove seeds; then chop.
½	green bell pepper	
¼	red onion	Chop green pepper and onion.
1	jalapeño	Slice jalapeño in half and remove seeds; then chop.
	juice of 1 lime	
1	garlic clove, minced	Combine all ingredients in a food processor. Pulse until well blended.
¼	tsp salt	

Per ¼ cup serving: 15 calories, 0 g fat, 3 g carbohydrates, 1 g fiber, 1 g protein

Laura's Layered Taco Dip

My sister serves this dip at our annual Oscar-viewing party.
It's always a hit. Serve it with your choice of tortilla or corn chips.

Makes 8 servings

1½ cups Refried Beans
(page 128) or canned
refried beans

1 small can mild green
chiles, drained

¼ cup (1 small packet)
taco seasoning mix,
divided (double check
the ingredients to
make sure the mix
is safe)

¾ cup Chipotle
Guacamole
(page 22)

1 6-ounce container
plain coconut yogurt
(optional)

1 cup diced tomatoes
(if using canned,
drain them first)

4 scallions, white part
only, chopped

In a small bowl, combine beans, chiles, and
2 tablespoons taco seasoning mix.

Spread bean mixture in the bottom of a pie
plate or shallow bowl. Top bean mixture
with guacamole.

If using coconut yogurt, combine it with
2 tablespoons of taco seasoning. Top
guacamole with yogurt mixture.

Combine tomatoes and scallions. Put them
on top of dip.

Per serving: 103 calories, 5 g fat, 13 g carbohydrates, 5 g fiber, 4 g protein

Fruit Kabobs

I've never met a kid who didn't like fruit and didn't like food served up in a fun way. This snack combines both. You can use any variety of fresh fruit in your kabobs: melons, berries, and mango are all good choices. Let your imagination run wild!

Makes 4 skewers

⅓   cup pineapple chunks

⅓   cup strawberries

⅓   cup banana slices

⅓   cup honeydew chunks

Thread fruit chunks, alternating colors and shapes, onto 5-inch cocktail straws. (Straws don't have sharp ends, so even little snackers can enjoy this treat safely.)

Per serving: 26 calories, 0 g fat, 7 g carbohydrates, 1 g fiber, 0 g protein

Candied Pumpkin Seeds

This sweet treat makes a great holiday gift or party favor. They look pretty in clear bags tied with a ribbon.

Makes 1 cup (4 servings)

2	*tbsps maple syrup*
2	*tbsps packed brown sugar*
¼	*tsp salt*
1	*cup shelled pumpkin seeds (pepitas)*

Preheat oven to 375°F.

In a small saucepan, combine maple syrup, brown sugar, and salt. Heat over medium heat. Stir constantly until brown sugar is melted and mixture is foamy.

Add pumpkin seeds and stir until coated.

Spread pumpkin seeds on oiled cookie sheet. Bake for 10 minutes, stirring after 5 minutes. Remove from oven and cool completely; stir occasionally while cooling to prevent pumpkin seeds from sticking to pan.

Per ¼ cup: 348 calories, 24 g fat, 21 g carbohydrates, 2 g fiber, 19 g protein

Easiest Applesauce

You can make this applesauce with just 2 or 3 apples or with a lot more. I like to use an apple that balances sweet and tart, like Jonathan or Macintosh apples; sweeter apples, like Golden Delicious, will yield sweeter sauce, while tart apples, like Granny Smith, will yield tart sauce.

Makes 1¾ cups

4   *apples*

    dash of cinnamon (optional)

3   *cups water*

Peel, core, and roughly chop apples. Place apple chunks in saucepan or stockpot. Sprinkle on cinnamon, if using. Cover apples with water.

Bring water to a boil, lower heat to a simmer, and cook until apples are soft and starting to break apart. (Length of time will depend on size of chunks and how many apples you're using.)

For smooth applesauce (for baking or babies), process until smooth in a food processor or blender.

Per ¼ cup serving: 3 calories, 0 g fat, 8 g carbohydrates, 1 g fiber, 0 g protein

Blueberry Applesauce

The sweetness of this sauce will depend on the type of apples used. For a delicious variation, peaches or strawberries blend nicely with applesauce, too. Mixing granola into applesauce transforms this snack into a meal.

Makes 4 cups

5   *medium apples (the sweetness of Pink Lady, Braeburn, or Macintosh blends nicely with the tartness of blueberries)*

2   *cups frozen or fresh blueberries*

1½–2 cups water

Peel, core, and chop apples.

Combine apples and blueberries with water in medium saucepan.

Simmer for 20 minutes or until the apples are soft.

Puree in food processor or mash with a fork or potato masher.

Per 1 cup serving: 160 calories, 1 g fat, 42 g carbohydrates, 7 g fiber, 1 g protein

Baked Tortilla Chips

These chips are the perfect accompaniment to a bowl of hearty soup, like Split Pea Soup (page 70), and pair beautifully with salsa, hummus, or guacamole. I use commercially made corn tortillas instead of homemade to make these chips, because they work really well and make this a very quick and easy snack.

Makes 8 servings (about 80 chips)

canola oil in spray pump

10 *corn tortillas*

salt to taste

Preheat oven to 350°F.

Spray a large cookie sheet with canola oil.

Cut tortillas into 8 wedges each.

Spread tortilla wedges on cookie sheet in a single layer.

Spray tops of tortilla wedges with canola oil and season with salt.

Bake 13–15 minutes until golden and crispy.

Per 10 chip serving: 65 calories, 2 g fat, 11 g carbohydrates, 2 g fiber, 1 g protein

Cinnamon-Sugar Tortilla Crisps

These tortilla crisps make an easy, sweet snack to toss in a bag and bring with you when you're out and about. I use commercially made corn tortillas to make these chips instead of homemade.

Makes 6 servings (80 crisps)

canola oil in spray pump	Preheat oven to 350°F.
10 *corn tortillas*	Spray a large cookie sheet with canola oil.
1 *tbsp sugar*	Cut tortillas into 8 wedges each.
1 *tsp cinnamon*	Spread tortilla wedges on cookie sheet in a single layer.

In a small covered bowl or jar, combine sugar and cinnamon.

Spray tops of tortilla wedges with canola oil and sprinkle with cinnamon-sugar mixture. (Keep remaining cinnamon-sugar mixture in a sealed container until next time.)

Bake 13–15 minutes until golden and crispy.

Per serving: 103 calories, 2 g fat, 20 g carbohydrates, 3 g fiber, 2 g protein

Trail Mix

This nutritious snack will provide lots of energy for any activity.
If you are using unsalted seeds, add ½ teaspoon salt. Adding a
handful of chocolate chips will turn this into a decadent treat.

Makes 2 cups

½ cup pepitas
(pumpkin seeds)

½ cup sunflower seeds

½ cup dried cherries

½ cup raisins

3 tbsps allergy-free
chocolate chips
(optional)

Combine all ingredients.

Per ½ cup serving: 307 calories, 19 g fat, 32 g carbohydrates, 31 g fiber, 9 g protein

Granola Bars

One of the challenges of feeding someone with food allergies is finding nutritious snacks to take on the go. These mini bars are packed full of nutrition and great taste. Cooking these bars in muffin papers serves two purposes. One, they are easy to take with you, and two, the papers keep the crumbs from falling out, so you can savor every last bite. Freeze extra bars so you can have a tasty snack whenever you want it.

Makes 36 bars

2	tbsps ground flaxseed
⅓	cup sunflower seed butter
¼	cup oat flour
⅓	cup apple juice
1	recipe Granola (page 164), minus the fruit
½	cup dried, sweetened cranberries
½	cup raisins

Preheat oven to 350°F.

In a large bowl, combine flaxseed with ¼ cup water. Add sunflower seed butter, oat flour, and apple juice; stir to combine. Mix in granola, cranberries, and raisins.

Line standard muffin tins with paper liners. Scoop a heaping tablespoon (about 1½ tablespoons) of mixture into each paper. Press down with damp fingers.

Bake 18–20 minutes, or until golden brown. Cool completely.

Per bar: 69 calories, 3 g fat, 10 g carbohydrates, 1 g fiber, 2 g protein

Emergency Sweet Snack Mix

Sometimes you need a sweet snack . . . NOW! When the craving hits, you can substitute any dried fruit for the raisins in this recipe— dried cherries are an especially good choice.

Makes 4 servings

1   cup crispy rice cereal

½   cup raisins

¼   cup allergy-free
    chocolate chips

Combine all ingredients in a bowl.

Per serving: 145 calories, 4 g fat, 29 g carbohydrates, 1 g fiber, 2 g protein

Seasoned Popcorn

My friend Julie taught me how to make great popcorn—and it's so easy. All you have to do is put the kernels in a brown paper bag, roll the top over, and put the bag in the microwave. Cook for 3 to 4 minutes or until the popping slows down...and enjoy perfect popcorn. Adding prepared seasoned salt (most grocery stores stock several brands) and nutritional yeast imparts a rich, almost cheesy flavor to this movie-favorite snack.

Makes 3 cups

¾ tsp seasoned salt

¾ tsp nutritional yeast

3 cups popped popcorn

   canola oil spray

In a small bowl, combine seasoned salt and nutritional yeast.

Spray popcorn with oil.

Toss with seasonings.

Per 1 cup serving: 33 calories, 0 g fat, 6 g carbohydrates, 1 g fiber, 1 g protein

SALADS & SOUPS

....

Salads and soups are delicious and rich in vegetables and proteins, herbs and flavor. They are also great additions to any welcoming kitchen. You can throw a casual party with a menu that's delicious and interesting for all your guests by serving two or three soups or salads together. They also make a great centerpiece for a weeknight dinner, and since you can usually make them ahead of time, you'll be able to get dinner on the table in a flash!

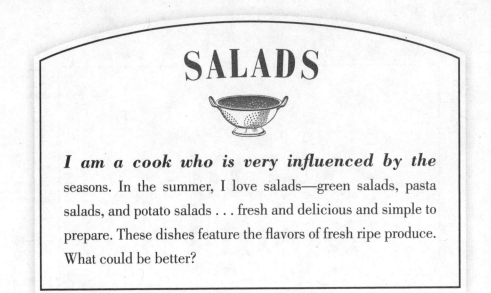

SALADS

I am a cook who is very influenced by the seasons. In the summer, I love salads—green salads, pasta salads, and potato salads . . . fresh and delicious and simple to prepare. These dishes feature the flavors of fresh ripe produce. What could be better?

Farmers' Market Salad

Let the season's bounty be your guide for this salad. Grape or cherry tomatoes, snap peas, or green beans are just a few tasty options to switch in and out of this salad.

Makes 4 servings

1   *bunch asparagus (about 10 spears)*

1   *large tomato*

2   *tbsps fresh basil, chopped*

¼   *onion, chopped*

1   *cup (8 ounces) garbanzo beans (either cooked or canned and rinsed)*

2   *tbsps Balsamic Vinaigrette (page 56)*

Trim tough ends of asparagus. Steam asparagus over medium heat for two to three minutes until crisp-tender. Rinse under cold water to stop cooking and to chill. Cut asparagus into 1½-inch pieces.

Combine asparagus, tomato, basil, onion, and beans; toss with vinaigrette.

Per serving: 107 calories, 3 g fat, 18 g carbohydrates, 4 g fiber, 4 g protein

Ruby Coleslaw

Add a punch of color to your plate with this vibrant salad—the perfect companion to Stuffed Baked Potatoes (page 96) or alongside Veggie Loaf (page 85).

Makes 10 servings

½   large purple cabbage

2   carrots, peeled

½   onion

¾   cup prepared cranberry sauce

¼   cup olive oil

½   tsp salt

    freshly ground pepper

1   tbsp agave nectar

3   tbsps apple cider vinegar

Shred cabbage. Finely chop carrots and onion. Combine vegetables in a large bowl.

In a small bowl, thoroughly combine cranberry sauce, olive oil, salt, pepper, agave nectar, and vinegar.

Toss slaw with dressing. Let coleslaw rest for at least an hour before serving.

Per serving: 109 calories, 6 g fat, 15 g carbohydrates, 2 g fiber, 1 g protein

Tomato Cucumber Salad

The vegetables in this refreshing salad will give off some liquid, so serve it up with a.slotted spoon. It's a good substitution for coleslaw and adds a satisfying crunch to sandwich wraps—just heat a corn tortilla or gluten-free wrap, spread with hummus, and top with a spoonful of the salad.

Makes 2 servings

Salads & Soups

1	medium tomato	Cut tomato in quarters and remove seeds. Cut in thin slices.
1	medium cucumber	
¼	sweet onion (Vidalia or Walla Walla)	Peel cucumber. Cut cucumber in half; scoop out seeds.
¼	cup canola oil	Thinly slice cucumber and onion.
2	tbsps white wine vinegar	In a medium bowl, combine oil, vinegar, agave nectar, salt, and thyme.
1	tsp agave nectar	
¼	tsp salt	Toss vegetables with dressing.
¾	tsp fresh thyme	

Per serving: 284 calories, 27 g fat, 9 g carbohydrates, 2 g fiber, 1 g protein

Deconstructed Guacamole Salad

Serve this creamy, tangy salad with a Country Corn Muffin
(page 148) for a fresh-tasting summer lunch.

Makes 2 servings

2	plum tomatoes
1	tbsp plus 1 tsp chopped red onion
1	avocado
1	tbsp cilantro, finely chopped
2	tsps lemon juice
1	tsp olive oil
⅛	tsp salt
⅛	tsp cayenne

Thinly slice tomatoes and arrange on two
plates. Top each plate of tomatoes with
chopped onion.

Cut avocado in half and remove seed.
Run a knife around the inside edge of the
avocado halves. Slice the avocado in the
skin lengthwise and then widthwise.
Turn the avocado inside out, and drop
the cubes onto the tomatoes and onion
on the two plates.

In a small bowl, combine cilantro, lemon
juice, olive oil, salt, and cayenne.

Drizzle dressing over salads.

TIP If you want to take the bite out
of raw onions, soak them in ice water for a
few minutes.

Per serving: 196 calories, 17 g fat, 12 g carbohydrates, 8 g fiber, 3 g protein

Potato Apple Salad

Yukon Gold potatoes work especially well in this nicely textured salad.

Makes 6 servings

Salads & Soups

4   potatoes
    (Yukon Gold work
    nicely)

1   tbsp German-style
    mustard

2   tbsps olive oil

1   tbsp lemon juice

¼   cup chopped
    sweet onion

1   apple, chopped

Peel and chop potatoes. Place chopped potatoes in a medium saucepan. Fill with water to cover potatoes. Bring to a boil.

Cook until chunks are fork-tender. Drain and rinse under cold water.

In a bowl, thoroughly combine mustard, olive oil, and lemon juice.

Toss potatoes, onion, and apple with dressing.

Per serving: 173 calories, 5 g fat, 31 g carbohydrates, 3 g fiber, 3 g protein

Roasted Potato Salad

Pair this delicious side salad with Jerk Portabella Mushroom (page 101) and Herbed Broccoli Salad (page 50) for a glorious al fresco dinner.

Makes 6 servings

6	medium russet, red, or golden potatoes
½	red onion
2	tbsps olive oil
¼	tsp salt
	freshly ground pepper to taste
¼	cup vegan white wine
1	tbsp lemon juice
1	tbsp finely chopped dill

Preheat oven to 450°F.

Scrub potatoes, quarter, and slice ½-inch thick.

Thinly slice onion.

Toss potatoes, onion, olive oil, salt, and pepper. Spread vegetables onto a cookie sheet and bake for 20 minutes, tossing halfway through.

While vegetables are cooking, mix white wine and lemon juice in a small saucepan. Cook until reduced by half.

Toss cooked vegetables with wine mixture and dill.

Serve at room temperature or warmed.

Per serving: 221 calories, 5 g fat, 40 g carbohydrates, 3 g fiber, 5 g protein

Summertime Corn Salad

If you use super-fresh summer corn, you don't even need to cook it before using it in this colorful salad—and it gives you a great excuse to visit your local farmers' market.

Makes 8 servings

2   *ears of corn (or about 2 cups thawed, frozen corn)*

¼   *cup chopped red onion*

½   *cup chopped green pepper*

½   *cup black beans, drained and rinsed*

½   *cup salsa— Lime-Lover's Salsa (page 29) or bottled salsa*

Cut corn kernels from cobs. Toss all ingredients together.

Chill before serving.

Per serving: 37 calories, 0 g fat, 8 g carbohydrates, 2 g fiber, 2 g protein

Herbed Broccoli Salad

In the winter, you can use dried herbs, substitute olive oil for the lemon juice, and serve the broccoli as a warm vegetable side dish.

Makes 6 servings

3	cups steamed broccoli florets
1	tsp lemon juice
1	tbsp finely chopped fresh basil (or 1 tsp dried)
1	tbsp finely chopped fresh oregano (or 1 tsp dried)
1	tbsp finely chopped fresh chives (or 1 tsp dried)
1	tbsp finely chopped fresh thyme (or 1 tsp dried)

Toss all ingredients together. Serve either chilled or warm.

Per serving: 7 calories, 0 g fat, 1 g carbohydrates, 1 g fiber, 1 g protein

Fruity Carrot Salad

This salad is an updated and improved version of the basic carrot, raisin, and mayonnaise salad that I loved as a kid. It goes really well with Lentil Burgers (page 77) or Black Bean Burgers (page 76).

Makes 4 servings

4	carrots
1	pear
½	cup sweetened dried cranberries
¼	cup vanilla coconut-based yogurt
½	tsp agave nectar

Peel carrots. Continue to use the vegetable peeler to slice carrots into ribbons.

Peel the pear or not, according to your preference. Chop the pear.

Combine carrots, pear, and cranberries in a large bowl.

In a small bowl, combine yogurt and agave nectar; add to carrot mixture.

Toss carrot mixture thoroughly with dressing.

Per serving: 121 calories, 2 g fat, 28 g carbohydrates, 4 g fiber, 1 g protein

Taco Salad

Perfect for warm weather, the cool vegetables in Taco Salad make it a light, but substantial summer dinner.

Makes 4 servings

2   cups vegetable broth

½   packet taco seasoning

3   tbsp olive oil, divided

1   cup kasha (roasted buckwheat)

1   cup chopped onion

2   large diced tomatoes, divided, OR 1 cup canned, drained tomatoes and 1 large fresh tomato, diced

1   cup chopped mild chiles, drained

3   cups chopped mixed lettuces

1   medium red onion, chopped

1   cup of corn (either defrosted frozen corn or lightly steamed fresh corn cut from the cob)

½   cup black olives, sliced

¼   cup fresh cilantro, chopped

2   avocados, peeled and cut in ¾-inch chunks

1   cup broken tortilla chips

1   cup salsa

In a small saucepan, bring vegetable broth, taco seasoning, and 2 tablespoons olive oil to a boil. Add kasha; reduce heat, cover, and simmer 10 minutes.

In a medium frying pan, heat the remaining tablespoon of olive oil over medium-high heat. Add onion, 1 diced tomato or 1 cup canned, drained tomatoes, and chiles. Sauté until soft. Add kasha to vegetables. Stir to combine.

Combine lettuces, remaining diced fresh tomato, red onion, corn, black olives, and cilantro. Toss to mix. Divide lettuce mixture into four bowls or plates. Top with kasha filling. Add avocado. Top with tortilla chips and salsa to taste.

Per serving: 654 calories, 33 g fat, 85 g carbohydrates, 15 g fiber, 14 g protein

SALAD DRESSINGS

There's no right or wrong way to put together a green salad. Some folks (like me) love a chopped salad where everything is bite-sized. Others prefer a fancier presentation. There's no limit to what you can toss into a salad.

My mom is the unofficial Salad Queen. She tosses different lettuces with orange peppers, scallions, raisins or sweetened cranberries, artichoke hearts, hearts of palm, tomatoes, cucumbers, and more. Then she adds lots of herbs before tossing the salad with the dressing. Super Yum! When I'm making salad, I love to toss in sunflower seeds, pumpkin seeds, or garbanzo beans. Sliced fruit makes a really great addition, too. Clean out your fridge, pick one of the following dressings, and feast!

Red Wine and Lemon Vinaigrette

You can completely transform this dressing by adding finely chopped herbs. Try rosemary, basil, dill, cilantro, or chives.

Makes ½ cup

¼ cup olive oil

⅛ cup red wine vinegar

⅛ cup lemon juice

   salt & pepper

Combine all ingredients in a lidded jar. Shake well.

Per 1 tbsp serving: 123 calories, 14 g fat, 1 g carbohydrates, 0 g fiber, 0 g protein

Lemon Dill Salad Dressing

Brighten up steamed green beans or asparagus with a drizzle of this sunny dressing.

Makes ¾ cup

6   tbsps light coconut milk

¼   cup fresh lemon juice

¼   cup fresh dill, minced

Combine all ingredients in a small food processor and blend thoroughly.

Per 2 tbsp serving: 33 calories, 3 g fat, 2 g carbohydrates, 0 g fiber, 0 g protein

Creamy Asian Dressing

You can turn steamed pea pods into a fantastic salad by tossing them with water chestnuts, sliced scallions, and this lovely dressing.

Makes ¾ cup

4	tbsps sunflower seed butter	Combine all ingredients. Mix well.
4	tbsps orange juice	
4	tbsps light coconut milk	
2	cloves garlic, minced	

Per 2 tbsp serving: 78 calories, 6 g fat, 5 g carbohydrates, 0 g fiber, 2 g protein

Agave Mustard Salad Dressing

This sweet and tangy dressing adds a boost of flavor to wraps and sandwiches, as well as salads.

Makes 5 tablespoons

1	tbsp agave nectar	Combine ingredients in a jar with a lid. Shake vigorously.
1	tbsp Dijon mustard	
2	tbsps apple cider vinegar	**TIP** Agave Mustard Salad Dressing also makes a great dip for cut-up bell peppers, cherry tomatoes, and broccoli.
1	tbsp canola oil	

Per 1 tbsp serving: 40 calories, 3 g fat, 3 g carbohydrates, 0 g fiber, 0 g protein

Balsamic Vinaigrette

This classic vinaigrette does double-duty as a salad dressing and a flavorful marinade for grilled vegetables. Simply toss the veggies with Balsamic Vinaigrette and let them sit either at room temperature or in the refrigerator for 15–30 minutes before grilling.

Makes ½ cup

¼ cup balsamic vinegar

¼ cup extra-virgin
    olive oil

    pinch of sugar

    salt & pepper

Combine all ingredients in a lidded jar. Shake well.

Per 1 tbsp serving: 67 calories, 7 g fat, 1 g carbohydrates, 0 g fiber, 0 g protein

SOUPS

Whenever I feel stuck in a menu routine, feeding my family variations of the same vegetables and proteins, I whip up a soup to jolt us back into diversified eating. Since soup is such a comforting vehicle, new or unfamiliar ingredients are usually much more welcome to my boys when they're in a brothy bowl. Something that would be completely ignored if it was standing alone on a plate gets gobbled up on a spoon, especially if there's a muffin to go along with it.

Gazpacho

Gazpacho, my brother-in-law Rob's favorite summer snack, crosses the line between salad and soup. It's cold and refreshing like a salad, but it's still a soup.

Makes 4 servings

4	roma (plum) tomatoes
½	green bell pepper
1	cucumber
1	jalapeño pepper
2	tbsps diced chives
1	tbsp lemon juice
1	tsp fresh thyme
¼	tsp salt

Seed and chop tomatoes.

Chop green pepper.

Peel and seed cucumber; then chop.

Remove seeds from jalapeño and dice.

Toss all ingredients together. Pour into a food processor or blender. Blend until very finely chopped and well blended.

Chill for at least an hour before serving.

Per 1 cup serving: 23 calories, 0 g fat, 5 g carbohydrates, 2 g fiber, 1 g protein

Throw-Together Tomato Soup

With some basic kitchen ingredients on hand, you can make a homey, delicious soup in very little time. You can replace the rice in this recipe with leftover grain, like quinoa, or pasta, or omit it altogether, for a basic, creamy tomato soup. Kids of any age will love a bowl of this soup served with a sandwich or a Beanadilla (page 73) for lunch or a light supper.

Makes 4 servings

1	tbsp olive oil
1	medium onion
2	garlic cloves
1	28-ounce can diced tomatoes
½	cup rice milk
1	cup cooked short-grain brown rice

Heat olive oil in a medium saucepan over medium heat. Chop onion, and smash garlic. Add to oil. Cook until soft, but not browned. Remove from heat.

Drain liquid from tomatoes. In a blender, puree tomatoes with garlic and onion.

Return mixture to the saucepan; stir in rice milk and rice.

Heat and serve.

Per 1 cup serving: 175 calories, 5 g fat, 31 g carbohydrates, 5 g fiber, 5 g protein

Vegetable Broth

To make this basic vegetable broth, use whatever vegetables you have on hand—any root vegetable, squash, or even greens will do. If you've ever wondered what to do with all the broccoli stalks you cut off when you're using just the crown of the broccoli in other recipes—you can use the stalks in this recipe. I often call for vegan bouillon in Welcoming Kitchen recipes because it's so convenient to use, but if you have some homemade Vegetable Broth on hand, in your fridge or freezer, you can use it instead. If your broth is unsalted, add a little salt to season the soup.

Makes 16 servings

1	large onion, peeled
4	garlic cloves, peeled
4	medium potatoes
5	carrots
4	celery ribs
2	zucchinis
4	broccoli stalks

Wash and coarsely chop all vegetables.

In a large stockpot, combine vegetables with 16 cups of water. Cover and boil for one hour.

Strain broth through a fine colander (or a colander lined with cheesecloth), pressing vegetables with the back of a spoon to remove as much liquid as possible.

Freeze any broth that you are not going to use in the next day or two.

Per 1 cup serving: 63 calories, 0 g fat, 15 g carbohydrates, 3 g fiber, 2 g protein

VARIATION

If you want the broth to be a ready-to-go soup base, add herbs and
seasonings before boiling.

1	*tsp dried basil*
1	*tsp dried oregano*
1	*tsp dried thyme*
2	*bay leaves*
½	*tsp salt*
1	*tsp black pepper*

Add seasonings to vegetables and water
before bringing to a boil. Remove and
discard bay leaves when you remove
vegetables from broth.

Salads & Soups

Creamy Corn Soup

If you decide to make this soup in a slow cooker (which works really well), add the rice milk after the soup has been blended.

Makes about 6 cups

2	ears of sweet corn	Cut corn from cob.
2	carrots	Peel and slice carrots.
1	large potato	Peel and chop potato, and chop green pepper and onion.
1	green pepper	
1	onion	
¾	tsp salt	Combine all vegetables, salt, pepper, and broth or water in a large stockpot.
	freshly ground black pepper	Bring to a boil, lower heat, and simmer for about 45 minutes, or until all the vegetables are tender.
4	cups vegetable broth or water	
1	cup rice milk	Working in batches, transfer most of the soup to a blender, and mix until smooth. The more soup you reserve from blending, the more texture the soup will have. If you blend it all, it will be a creamy, smooth soup.
		Mix rice milk into soup.

Per 1 cup serving: 137 calories, 1 g fat, 31 g carbohydrates, 3 g fiber, 4 g protein

Kitchen Sink Soup

You can use just about any vegetable you like in this soup. Try spinach or chard in place of collard greens or replace some of the potatoes or carrots with squash and turnips. A little hot sauce or red pepper flakes will boost the spiciness of this soup and give it a little extra heat.

Makes 18 cups

3	baking potatoes
3	sweet potatoes
3	carrots
2	onions
3	garlic cloves
1	medium bunch collard greens
4	cups diced tomatoes (or one 28-ounce can, not drained)
2	cups cooked garbanzo beans (or one 15-ounce can, drained and rinsed)
2	vegan bouillon cubes
10	cups water
	freshly ground pepper to taste
1	cup quinoa

Peel potatoes, carrots, and onions. Chop into roughly ½-inch chunks.

Smash the garlic.

Trim the spines from the collard greens. (Fold leaves in half and cut out the thick spine.) In a food processor, chop the collard greens into small bits.

In a large stock pot, combine chopped vegetables, tomatoes, beans, bouillon cubes, water, and pepper.

Rinse quinoa thoroughly with cool water to remove bitterness. Add to pot.

Bring to a boil, cover, and reduce heat to a simmer. Cook 45 minutes or until vegetables are tender.

Per 1 cup serving: 138 calories, 1 g fat, 29 g carbohydrates, 4 g fiber, 4 g protein

Creamy Cauliflower Soup

Sweet Potato Biscuits (page 161) make a delicious complement to this comforting soup.

Makes 8 servings

3	medium potatoes
1	medium head of cauliflower
1	leek
1	tbsp olive oil
4	cups water
2	tbsp nutritional yeast
1	tsp white pepper
½	tsp salt
½	tsp dry mustard
1	bay leaf

Dice potatoes and cauliflower.

Chop leek. In a large stockpot, sauté chopped leek in olive oil.

Add remaining ingredients; bring to a boil. Reduce heat to a simmer. Simmer about 30 minutes until potatoes and cauliflower are tender. Remove bay leaf.

Puree ⅔ of the soup in food processor or blender. Mix pureed soup back into pot with remaining soup.

Per 1 cup serving: 96 calories, 0 fat, 21 g carbohydrates, 4 g fiber, 4 g protein

Two-Potato Soup

When you need real comfort food, try this pretty, golden soup.
I first made it after we'd gotten over a stomach bug and were being
extra careful about what we ate. I knew our appetites were back
after we—and even the boys—ate up several bowls!

Makes 8 servings

5   medium sweet
    potatoes, peeled

10 Yukon Gold potatoes

3   vegan gluten-free
    bouillon cubes

    freshly ground pepper
    to taste

    splash of rice milk

Cut potatoes into chunks.

Add to a large stockpot with bouillon and
pepper. Add water to cover potatoes.

Bring to a boil. Reduce heat, cover, and
simmer until potatoes are very tender,
about 30 minutes.

Once potatoes are tender, transfer to a
blender (or use an immersion blender in
the pot), and blend until smooth.

Add rice milk until the soup has the
desired consistency.

TIP If you refrigerate any leftover
soup, thin it with a little more rice milk
before reheating.

Per 1 cup serving: 224 calories, 5 g fat, 51 g carbohydrates, 6 g fiber, 6 g protein

Creamy Broccoli Soup

My sons will swear up and down that they do not like broccoli, but if I make this soup, they eat it up! Although it isn't called for in this recipe, you can also toss in some soy-free, nut-free vegan cheese right before blending.

Makes 6 servings

2	tsps olive oil
1	stalk of celery, diced (OK to include the leaves)
1	carrot, peeled and diced
1	onion, diced
2	large garlic cloves, minced
1	bunch of broccoli (enough to make 4 cups chopped)
1	baking potato, peeled and diced
2	vegan bouillon cubes
2	cups water
1½	cups rice milk
	freshly ground pepper to taste

In a large stockpot, heat olive oil over medium-high heat. Add celery, carrot, onion, and garlic. Sauté until softened, about 3 minutes.

While vegetables are cooking, cut off the ends of the broccoli stalks. Peel the remaining stalks with a vegetable peeler, and chop the broccoli from flower to stem.

Add the broccoli and potato to the pot. Sauté for 2–3 minutes.

Add bouillon, water, rice milk, and pepper.

Bring to a boil. Reduce heat, cover, and simmer for 20–25 minutes until softened.

Blend soup with immersion blender or in a blender.

Per 1 cup serving: 95 calories, 2 g fat, 18 g carbohydrates, 1 g fiber, 3 g protein

Between the Seasons Soup

At that delicious time of year when the sun is still warm, but a cool breeze is starting to blow, you get the best of both worlds: the end of summer's bounty and the beginning of autumn's heartier offerings. Depending on how much water you use, this recipe, which celebrates the between season, works equally well as a soup or a stew. You can make the recipe in a slow cooker or in a soup pot on the stove. The quantities for vegetables are approximate. If you use two small green peppers instead of a medium-sized green pepper, it makes no difference; the soup will taste just as good.

Makes 8 servings

	kernels from 3 ears of corn	1	tsp cumin
1	medium green pepper	1	tsp salt
1	medium zucchini	½	tsp chili powder
5	small baking potatoes	¼	tsp cinnamon
2	cups cooked lima beans	1	6-ounce can tomato paste
1	small or medium onion		water to cover vegetables (approximately 6 cups)
1	butternut squash, peeled and seeds removed		
2	jalapeños, seeds & stems removed	2	cups chopped greens (chard, kale, collard, or spinach)

Chop all vegetables. Combine all ingredients except greens in a slow cooker. Cook on low for 6 hours.

Add chopped greens to hot soup; stir to combine. Let greens soften in soup for a few minutes before serving.

Per 1 cup serving: 186 calories, 1 g fat, 41 g carbohydrates, 6 g fiber, 8 g protein

Chili

Chili is great for all kinds of casual get-togethers, like the Super Bowl and birthday parties, and makes a cozy family supper in the autumn. This recipe is easy and makes a lot, so if you serve it for a weeknight dinner, you can freeze half for another time. I like to serve chili with chopped tomatoes, onions, and avocado on top. You can also use crushed tortilla or corn chips as a topping.

Makes 8 servings

2   cups vegetable broth

4   tbsps olive oil, divided

1   cup kasha (roasted buckwheat)

3   medium onions, chopped

3   cloves of garlic, minced

2   serrano peppers, minced

1   jalapeño pepper, minced
    (optional)

½   cup chili powder

1   tsp ground cumin

1   tsp dried oregano

4–5 cups diced tomatoes
    (2 20-ounce cans, drained)

1   15-ounce can kidney beans or
    mixed beans for chili, drained,
    and rinsed

½   tsp sugar

In a small saucepan, bring vegetable broth and 2 tablespoons olive oil to a boil. Add kasha, reduce heat, cover, and simmer 10 minutes.

In a large saucepan or stockpot, heat 2 tablespoons olive oil over medium heat. Add onions, garlic, and peppers. Sauté until soft.

Add chili powder, cumin, and oregano. Stir until spices are absorbed.

Add tomatoes, beans, sugar, and kasha.

Simmer uncovered for 20–30 minutes.

Per 1 cup serving: 286 calories, 9 g fat, 47 g carbohydrates, 9 g fiber, 9 g protein

Lentil Soup

If you use a food processor to dice the vegetables in this easy recipe for lentil soup, it can be prepared in minutes. You can also use 7½ cups of vegetable broth if you prefer it to bouillon cubes and water. Add salt to taste if the vegetable broth is low-salt or salt-free.

Makes 8 servings

2   tbsps olive oil

3   garlic cloves

1½ cups diced onions

7½ cups water

3   vegan bouillon cubes

2   cups diced carrots

1   cup diced celery

1   cup lentils, picked over and rinsed

2   cups diced tomatoes with liquid (either fresh or canned)

    black pepper to taste

In a large stockpot, heat olive oil over medium heat. Add garlic and onion. Cook until soft and fragrant.

Add water and remaining ingredients.

Bring to a boil. Reduce heat; simmer uncovered for 45 minutes.

Per 1 cup serving: 155 calories, 4 g fat, 23 g carbohydrates, 9 g fiber, 8 g protein

Split Pea Soup

Chipotle peppers bring the heat to this Lutz family favorite. Using a slow cooker makes this already easy dish a snap!

Makes 10 servings

1	medium onion, chopped
1	large carrot, chopped
3	medium baking potatoes, chopped
2	chipotle peppers in adobo sauce, minced
8	cups water
2	cups split peas, rinsed and picked over
¼	tsp allspice
¼	tsp salt

Combine all ingredients in a large stockpot.

Bring to a boil, reduce heat to a simmer, cover, and cook 45 minutes.

Soup is done when vegetables are tender, soup is thick, and split peas are tender.

Per 1 cup serving: 196 calories, 1 fat, 38 g carbohydrates, 12 g fiber, 13 g protein

LUNCHES & DINNERS

....

The recipes in this chapter work equally well for lunch or dinner. When you're feeding folks who have restricted diets, lunch can seem tricky, but once you start thinking outside the box, you'll discover all kinds of options: Soups and salads are a good fit at noon, but so are wraps, leftovers, and light entrees. Along with the recipes in this section, consider adding muffins, coconut-based yogurt with granola, trail mix with fruit, celery sticks with sunflower-seed butter, and refried beans with tortilla chips to the menu.

GRAINS & BEANS

No, we're not talking about the plain old rice and beans of the 1970s. There are many great uses for these nutrient-rich staples! Nutty brown rice or creamy risotto or hearty kasha—these basic components can easily be combined with other tasty ingredients to make some crowd-pleasing favorites. (Who would have thought you could make a great-textured, meat-free sausage without either tofu or wheat?) Take a new look at these economical pantry staples and welcome them into your kitchen!

Beanadillas

These hearty bean-filled tortillas make a great alternative to quesadillas. Serve with Lime-Lover's Salsa (page 29) and/or Chipotle Guacamole (page 22).

Makes 6 servings

1   cup Refried Beans (page 128) or use canned vegetarian refried beans—of course, check the label

12 Corn Tortillas (page 159) or use packaged tortillas

1   cup shredded soy- and nut-free vegan cheese (optional)

Preheat oven to 200°F.

Spread 2–3 tablespoons refried beans on a corn tortilla. Top with cheese, if using. Top with another tortilla.

Heat a dry skillet over a medium-high flame. Cook beanadillas, one at a time, for 2–3 minutes until heated through, turning at least once to ensure even cooking.

Keep warm in oven until all are done cooking.

Per serving: 174 calories, 4 fat, 31 g carbohydrates, 5 g fiber, 6 g protein

Guacamole Salad Wraps

Sometimes you really want a sandwich instead of a salad. Adding black beans and corn tortillas to Deconstructed Guacamole Salad transforms a tasty salad into a great wrap.

Makes 4 servings

1   recipe Deconstructed Guacamole Salad (page 46)

½   cup cooked black beans (canned are fine; just be sure to rinse and drain before using)

4   corn tortillas

Chop tomatoes in salad. Mix all salad ingredients together.

Add black beans to salad. Mix together.

Warm tortillas in a dry frying pan.

Divide filling among the tortillas and wrap them up.

Per serving: 180 calories, 10 g fat, 22 g carbohydrates, 7 g fiber, 5 g protein

Sloppy Joes

Lentils make the perfect foundation for this delicious variation on the classic Sloppy Joe. Serve over a slice of gluten-free Beer Bread (page 156), Biscuits (page 160), Creamy Polenta (page 105), or baked potatoes.

Makes 6 servings

1	cup dried lentils, rinsed and picked over
4	cups water
1	medium onion
1	medium green bell pepper
2	cloves garlic, pressed or finely minced
1	tbsp olive oil
1¼	cups ketchup
1	tbsp prepared yellow mustard
⅛–¼	tsp cayenne pepper

Combine lentils and water in medium saucepan. Simmer gently with lid tilted for about 40 minutes.

Finely chop onion and bell pepper. Press garlic with a garlic press. Heat olive oil over medium heat. Sauté onion, pepper, and garlic until slightly soft.

Add drained lentils, ketchup, mustard, and cayenne.

Per serving: 199 calories, 3 g fat, 36 g carbohydrates, 11 g fiber, 10 g protein

Black Bean Burgers

For a really great sandwich, top these burgers with a little Chipotle Guacamole (page 22), sliced tomato, and onion.

Makes 4 servings

1   15-ounce can black beans, drained and rinsed

¼   cup prepared salsa

¼   cup corn kernels (either fresh or frozen and thawed)

¼   cup chopped red onion

¼   cup cornmeal

1   tsp canola oil

Mash black beans with a potato masher or fork. Mix in salsa, corn, onion, and cornmeal. Form into 4 patties.

Heat canola oil in a small skillet. Cook burgers in hot pan, cooking 2–3 minutes per side.

Per serving: 127 calories, 2 g fat, 23 g carbohydrates, 7 g fiber, 6 g protein

Lentil Burgers

Serve these burgers with Biscuits (page 160), a slice of gluten-free Beer Bread (page 156), or Corn Tortillas (page 159). Their hearty warmth is sure to please anyone looking for a substantial sandwich.

Makes 6 burgers

1 cup dried lentils

5 cups plus 5 tbsps water, divided

2 tbsps flaxseed meal

2 cloves garlic, minced

½ tsp pepper sauce (like Tabasco)

¼ cup cornmeal

¼ tsp salt

freshly ground pepper to taste

2 tsps olive oil, divided

Pick over and rinse dried lentils. Combine lentils with 5 cups of water in a medium saucepan. Bring to a boil; reduce heat and cook for 40 minutes with lid tilted to let out steam. Transfer cooked lentils to a large bowl.

In a small bowl, combine flaxseed meal with 5 tablespoons water. Add flaxseed slurry to lentils.

Add garlic, pepper sauce, cornmeal, salt, and pepper. Combine thoroughly. Form into patties.

Heat 1 teaspoon olive oil in a medium skillet. Cook two patties at a time for two minutes per side. (If you cover the skillet while the burgers are cooking, they will be sure to cook through.)

Lunches & Dinners

Per serving: 162 calories, 3 g fat, 25 g carbohydrates, 11 g fiber, 9 g protein

Nachos

With just the right combination of gooey mess and crispy crunch, nachos are the ultimate junk food. Who wouldn't devour a lunch that feels like a treat?

Makes 3 servings

1 cup Refried Beans (page 128) or use canned vegetarian refried beans

¼ cup vegetable broth

2½ cups tortilla chips

½ cup shredded vegan cheese (soy-free, nut-free)

4 scallions, chopped

¼ cup black olives, sliced

1 medium tomato, chopped

1 can jalapeño slices

½ cup Lime-Lover's Salsa (page 29)

½ cup Chipotle Guacamole (page 22)

Preheat broiler.

Thin refried beans by adding vegetable broth, 1 tablespoon at a time, until desired consistency. The beans should be thin, but not runny.

Spread chips on a cookie sheet or baking pan. Top with vegan cheese. Top with beans.

Broil for 30 seconds, or until cheese is melted, beans are heated, and chips are crispy, but not burned.

Transfer chips to a serving platter.

Top with remaining ingredients.

Per serving: 441 calories, 21 g fat, 57 g carbohydrates, 12 g fiber, 11 g protein

Baked Beans

Serve these sweet and savory beans with Country Corn Muffins
(page 148) and crisp Tomato Cucumber Salad (page 45).

Makes 6 servings

2	15-ounce cans Great Northern beans, drained and rinsed
⅓	cup blackstrap molasses
2	cups diced tomatoes
2	tbsps brown sugar
1	chopped onion
2	tbsps Dijon mustard

Preheat oven to 375°F.

Mix together all ingredients. Bake in a covered casserole for 2 hours.

Lunches & Dinners

Per serving: 246 calories, 1 g fat, 51 g carbohydrates, 8 g fiber, 11 g protein

Italian Lasagna

The idea of a dairy-free lasagna that does not rely on tofu might at first sound strange, but the combination of acorn squash and Great Northern beans creates a creamy, comforting filling for this classic, Italian-influenced casserole. You can cut down on the prep time for this dish by baking the squash either earlier in the day or the day before making the lasagna.

Makes 6 servings

1   acorn squash

1   15-ounce can Great Northern beans, drained but not rinsed

1½ tbsps fresh basil

1½ tbsps fresh sage

2   garlic cloves

    salt & pepper

3   cups chunky tomato sauce—either Easy Tomato Basil Sauce (page 117), Roasted Tomato Sauce (page 122), or chunky bottled sauce

8   sheets no-bake rice lasagna

Preheat oven to 350°F.

Cut acorn squash in half and remove seeds. Place cut side down in baking pan and add water until it is 1½ inches deep in the pan. Bake until squash is soft, 50–60 minutes. Scoop squash flesh from skin.

In food processor or blender, combine squash, beans, basil, sage, garlic, salt, and pepper.

In a lasagna pan, layer tomato sauce, lasagna sheets, and squash filling, beginning and ending with sauce.

Bake 1 hour.

Per serving: 334 calories, 4 g fat, 65 g carbohydrates, 12 g fiber, 11 g protein

Mexican Lasagna

Loaded with rice, beans, and veggies, this take on lasagna makes a filling entrée for a family dinner or a casual meal for company.

Makes 6 servings

2   scant cups short-grain brown rice

4   cups water

1   bunch spinach

1   tbsp olive oil

1   garlic clove, minced

1   cup chopped red onion

1   cup corn, either fresh or frozen

1   4-ounce can diced mild green chiles, drained

3   cups tomato sauce, divided

1   cup salsa

2   cups Refried Beans (page 128) or 1 15-ounce can

12 corn tortillas

Preheat oven to 375°F.

Combine brown rice and water in a medium saucepan. Bring to a boil, cover, and simmer over low heat for 40 minutes.

Finely chop spinach (if using a food processor, add a little water to make a paste).

While rice is cooking, heat olive oil in a medium skillet. Sauté garlic. Add red onion, corn, and chiles; cook until onion is soft.

When rice is finished cooking, stir in chopped spinach, sautéed vegetables, and 1 cup tomato sauce. Combine remaining tomato sauce and salsa.

Spread a layer of salsa mixture on the bottom of a 9-inch baking pan. Top with a layer of tortillas. Spread beans on tortillas. Top with rice. Repeat layers of salsa mixture, tortillas, beans, and rice. Finish with a layer of sauce.

Bake uncovered for 45 minutes.

Per serving: 580 calories, 9 g fat, 111 g carbohydrates, 16 g fiber, 17 g protein

Middle Eastern Lentils and Rice

This simple dish is one of our family's favorite go-to comfort foods. It's quick and easy to prepare, and we almost always have the ingredients on hand. My boys eat it wrapped in tortillas—a Middle Eastern burrito.

Makes 3 servings

1 cup short-grain brown rice

2¼ cups water

½ cup dried lentils, rinsed and picked over

¼ tsp cumin

1 vegan bouillon cube

3 tbsps olive oil, divided

1 onion, finely chopped

freshly ground black pepper, to taste

In a medium saucepan, combine rice, water, lentils, cumin, and bouillon) with 1½ tablespoons olive oil. Bring to a boil. Reduce heat, cover pan, and simmer on low heat for 40 minutes.

While the rice is cooking, heat remaining olive oil over high heat.

Fry the onion until golden brown.

Fluff rice and lentils; serve on a platter topped with onions and pepper.

Per 1 cup serving: 480 calories, 16 g fat, 71 g carbohydrates, 13 g fiber, 14 g protein

Tacos

Although buckwheat tacos might sound a little unusual at first, kasha makes a great base for a taco filling. Go on, give it a try!

Makes 4 servings

2	cups vegetable broth
½	packet taco seasoning
3	tbsps olive oil, divided
1	cup roasted buckwheat (kasha)
1	cup chopped onion
1	cup diced tomatoes (drained if you're using canned tomatoes)
1	can chopped mild chiles, drained
8	corn tortillas (or taco shells)

For toppings, assemble bowls of the following (or other toppings of your choice):

chopped lettuce or cabbage

tomatoes

onions

black olives

salsa and/or guacamole for garnish

In a small saucepan, bring vegetable broth, taco seasoning, and 2 tablespoons olive oil to a boil. Add kasha, reduce heat, cover, and simmer 10 minutes.

In a medium frying pan, heat remaining tablespoon of olive oil over medium-high heat. Add onion, tomatoes, and chiles. Sauté until soft.

Add kasha to vegetables. Stir to combine.

Heat taco shells or tortillas. Fill with kasha filling. Top with chopped lettuce, tomatoes, onions, and black olives. Garnish with salsa and/or guacamole.

Per serving: 405 calories, 13 g fat, 65 g carbohydrates, 7 g fiber, 10 g protein

Quinoa and Beans

Since quinoa cooks quickly, this satisfying dinner can be on the table in less than half an hour.

Makes 6 servings

1 cup quinoa

2¼ cups vegetable broth, divided

1 tbsp olive oil

2 cups torn rainbow chard

1 cup cooked garbanzo beans, drained and rinsed

½ tsp hot sauce (like Tabasco)

Thoroughly rinse quinoa under cool water. (It can have a bitter taste if not well rinsed.) Bring 2 cups vegetable broth to a boil. Add quinoa, cover, and reduce heat to a simmer. Cook 15 minutes, or until liquid is absorbed and the outer germ separates.

While quinoa is cooking, heat remaining vegetable broth and olive oil in a medium skillet over medium-high heat. Add chard to skillet, and cook until it's wilted.

Add chard, garbanzo beans, and hot sauce to cooked quinoa. Stir thoroughly to combine.

Per serving: 106 calories, 4 g fat, 15 g carbohydrates, 3 g fiber, 4 g protein

Veggie Loaf

For a comforting family dinner, serve Dill Carrots (page 131) and Old-Fashioned Mashed Potatoes (page 132) with Veggie Loaf.

Makes 6 servings

2	tbsps flaxseed meal
2¼	cups water
2	tbsps olive oil, divided
1	large carrot, chopped
1	medium onion, chopped
2	garlic cloves, minced
1	small bunch of kale, minced
2	vegan bouillon cubes
1	cup kasha (roasted buckwheat)
2	tsps poultry seasoning
	canola oil spray

Preheat oven to 350°F.

In a small bowl, combine flaxseed meal and ¼ cup water.

Heat 1 tablespoon olive oil in a large sauté pan. Add carrot, onion, and garlic; sauté for 2 minutes. Add kale; sauté for another 3–5 minutes. Remove from heat.

While vegetables are cooking, bring 2 cups water, bouillon cubes, and 1 tablespoon olive oil to a boil. Add kasha to boiling water and simmer for 10 minutes.

Add kasha and flaxseed slurry to the vegetables and mix in poultry seasoning.

Spray a square baking pan with canola oil. Spread mixture in pan. Bake 45 minutes.

Per serving: 188 calories, 6 g fat, 29 g carbohydrates, 3 g fiber, 6 g protein

Artichoke-Portabella Risotto

There is something about the combination of artichokes and mushrooms that completely satisfies me. This is a company-worthy entrée that shouldn't be saved just for entertaining.

Makes 4 servings

4	cups vegetable broth
1	shallot
2	portabella mushroom caps
6–8	artichoke hearts
2	tbsps olive oil
1	cup arborio rice
	freshly ground pepper
½	cup vegan white wine

In a saucepan, simmer vegetable broth.

Quarter and then thinly slice shallot.

Remove gills from mushroom caps by scraping with a spoon. Thinly slice caps and then chop into ½-inch pieces.

Roughly chop artichoke hearts.

Heat olive oil in a large skillet or sauté pan over medium-high heat. Add shallot and artichoke hearts; sauté until soft. Add chopped mushrooms; sauté until soft. Add rice and pepper to vegetables. Stir thoroughly. Add wine, and cook until wine is absorbed.

Add broth to rice mixture, one ladleful at a time. Stir until liquid is absorbed, and then add another ladleful until all of the broth is absorbed and the rice is tender.

Per serving: 293 calories, 10 g fat, 46 g carbohydrates, 2 g fiber, 4 g protein

Spinach and Cherry Tomato Risotto

This colorful entrée is a festive choice for a holiday dinner. Serve it with Crostini (page 17) and Olivada (page 20) along with an elegant tossed salad.

Makes 4 servings

4	*cups vegetable broth*
2	*tbsps olive oil*
2	*garlic cloves, minced*
1½	*cups chopped spinach (if using frozen spinach, thaw and dry before cooking)*
1	*cup arborio rice*
½	*cup vegan white wine*
1	*cup cherry tomatoes*

In a medium saucepan, heat vegetable broth over medium heat; keep at a low simmer.

Heat olive oil in a large skillet or sauté pan.
Add garlic and sauté until soft.
Add spinach and cook until wilted.
Add rice and coat with oil.
Add wine and cook until mostly absorbed.

Add one ladleful of broth. Stir until absorbed. Continue adding broth one ladleful at a time until all of the broth has been absorbed.

Slice tomatoes in half. Toss tomatoes in risotto, and heat together for a minute or two.

Lunches & Dinners

Per serving: 346 calories, 9 g fat, 54 g carbohydrates, 4 g fiber, 7 g protein

Pumpkin Risotto

This is a cheater's risotto since it cooks in the oven, rather than using the more labor-intensive stovetop method.

Makes 4 servings

1	tbsp olive oil
1	garlic clove
½	cup arborio rice
½	cup canned pumpkin
1½	cups vegetable broth
½	cup vegan white wine
6	artichoke hearts, quartered
½	cup garbanzo beans, drained and rinsed
	salt & pepper

Preheat oven to 350°F.

Combine olive oil and garlic in a small bowl. Microwave on high for 20 seconds. (Or heat garlic and olive oil in a small saucepan until garlic is fragrant, 1–2 minutes.) Remove garlic from oil and discard.

Rinse rice. Combine rice with remaining ingredients, including garlic-infused oil, in a covered oven-safe bowl or casserole.

Bake 1 hour, stir, and return to the oven for 15 more minutes.

Remove from oven, stir, and let sit for at least 5 minutes before serving.

Per serving: 235 calories, 6 g fat, 35 g carbohydrates, 4 g fiber, 5 g protein

Sausage Patties

You can rely on these delicious sausage patties to take center stage at brunch, but they can also be part of a hearty sandwich or dinner. Two chipotle peppers will yield a very spicy patty, one pepper will make a medium-spicy patty, and one-half will be pretty mild.

Makes 6 patties

2   cups water

1   cup kasha
     (roasted buckwheat)

1   vegan bouillon cube

½   cup Great Northern
     beans, either cooked
     or canned, and then
     drained and rinsed

2   chipotle peppers
     (from a can of
     chipotle peppers in
     adobo sauce)

¼   cup nutritional yeast

½   tsp onion powder

1   tsp dried oregano

2   tsps canola oil

Preheat oven to 350°F.

In a small saucepan, bring water to boil. Add kasha and a bouillon cube to boiling water, reduce heat, and cover. Simmer 10 minutes or until water is absorbed.

Thoroughly mash beans. Add 1½ cups cooked kasha to beans (use remaining kasha for another purpose). Finely chop chipotle peppers and add to kasha and beans. Add nutritional yeast, onion powder, and oregano to kasha and beans. Thoroughly mash together.

Lightly oil a six-muffin pan. Evenly divide the mixture among the six muffin cups. Lightly press down. Set muffin pan in a 9-inch by 13-inch pan. Add 1 inch of boiling water to outer pan. Cover with aluminum foil. Bake for 30 minutes.

Slide sausage patties out of muffin pan, and cool slightly. Heat canola oil in a medium skillet. Lightly fry patties on each side.

Per sausage patty: 177 calories, 3 g fat, 31 g carbohydrates, 51 g fiber, 11 g protein

Caribbean Black Bean Sauté

This complete one-bowl meal brings sunshine and a taste of the tropics to even the gloomiest day.

Makes 4 servings

2   medium sweet potatoes, peeled and chopped in 1-inch pieces

2   cloves garlic, minced

3   tbsps olive oil, divided

1   15-ounce can black beans or 2 cups cooked black beans

⅓   cup coconut milk

    ½-inch piece fresh ginger, peeled and minced

¼   tsp allspice

2   cups pineapple chunks (fresh or frozen)

1   small onion, chopped

¼   cup orange juice

    Tabasco to taste

4   cups cooked rice

Preheat oven to 400°F.

Toss sweet potatoes and garlic with 2 tablespoons olive oil. Roast sweet potatos on cookie sheet for 20 minutes.

While sweet potatoes are cooking, combine other ingredients plus 1 tablespoon olive oil in a sauté pan and cook over medium heat. Add cooked sweet potato mixture to beans.

If mixture is too dry, add water or more orange juice, 1 tablespoon at a time.

Serve over rice or quinoa.

Per serving: 272 calories, 5 g fat, 51 g carbohydrates, 8 g fiber, 10 g protein

VEGETABLES

Colorful, flavorful, beautiful . . . vegetables are an endless source of inspiration. Since they are naturally gluten-free, veggies can be a great starting point for the creation of delicious meals. My boys will often eat a vegetable as part of a complete dish although they would never eat it simply steamed or served alone. In the summer I love going to the farmers' market to see all the luscious, seasonal produce and then whipping up a fresh, fantastic dinner. I hope these recipes also inspire your creativity in the kitchen.

Quinoa-Stuffed Peppers

Serve Biscuits (page 160) with this delicious, messy dish so you can mop up every last bit!

Makes 4 servings

1   cup quinoa

2   cups water

1   vegan bouillon cube

½   onion, chopped

8   ounces button or cremini mushrooms, chopped

2   cloves garlic, minced

1   tbsp fresh minced basil or 1 tsp dried

1   tbsps fresh minced oregano or 1 tsp dried

½   tbsp fresh minced rosemary or ½ tsp dried

1   15-ounce can artichoke hearts, rinsed, drained, and chopped

2   tbsps olive oil

2   cups Easy Tomato Basil Sauce (page 117) or bottled sauce)

4   green peppers

Preheat oven to 350°F.

Rinse quinoa. Combine quinoa, 2 cups water, and bouillon cube in a saucepan. Bring to a boil, cover, and simmer for 10 minutes (quinoa is cooked when the outer germ separates).

While quinoa is cooking, sauté onion, mushrooms, garlic, herbs, and artichoke hearts in olive oil over medium heat, about 10 minutes. Combine quinoa and vegetables.

Spread ⅓ of the Easy Tomato Basil Sauce in the bottom of an 8-inch by 8-inch pan. Cut green peppers in half. Remove stems, seeds, and membranes. Stuff peppers with quinoa mixture. Place in sauce in pan. Spread remaining sauce over peppers.

Bake 40 minutes.

Per pepper: 412 calories, 18 g fat, 54 g carbohydrates, 8 g fiber, 10 g protein

Ratatouille

This zucchini and eggplant stew takes full advantage of garden-fresh produce. Serve it over polenta, quinoa, or pasta.

Makes 6 servings

2	tbsps olive oil
1	onion, chopped
3	garlic cloves, minced
1	zucchini, quartered and thinly sliced
1	green pepper, chopped
½	eggplant, quartered and thinly sliced
1	15-ounce can artichoke hearts, quartered
1	28-ounce can diced tomatoes, drained (or 2½ cups diced fresh tomatoes)
2	tbsps chopped fresh basil
¼	tsp red pepper flakes

Heat olive oil over medium heat in a large skillet or sauté pan. Add onion and garlic; sauté for one minute. Add remaining ingredients.

Cook over medium heat, stirring occasionally, for ½ hour.

Per serving: 142 calories, 10 fat, 14 g carbohydrates, 3 g fiber, 2 g protein

Italian Eggplant

This dish is similar to eggplant parmesan. It is a much healthier version, but just as tasty. It makes a delicious dish for special occasions, served with a side of gluten-free pasta dressed with olive oil and fresh herbs or one of the risottos from this book.

Makes 6 servings

1	large eggplant
	salt
1	cup cornmeal
1	tsp dried oregano or 1 tbsp fresh
1	tsp dried basil or 1 tbsp fresh
1	tsp dried rosemary or 1 tbsp fresh
2	tbsps olive oil
3	cups pasta sauce

Thinly slice eggplant (the slicing attachment on a food processor works well for this). Sprinkle eggplant slices with salt; set aside for 20 minutes; then rinse.

Preheat oven to 350°F.

Combine cornmeal and herbs in a large bowl. Mix in olive oil. Toss eggplant slices in cornmeal mixture.

In a lasagna pan, alternate layers of sauce and eggplant, beginning and ending with sauce.

Bake 50–60 minutes until sauce is bubbly and eggplant is tender when pierced with a fork.

Per serving: 273 calories, 9 g fat, 44 g carbohydrates, 8 g fiber, 5 g protein

Cheesy Broccoli Baked Potatoes

To be sure that you're using completely vegan, dairy-free cheese, try Welcoming Kitchen–friendly options like Daiya, which makes a great shredded cheese, and rice-based block or sliced cheeses made by Galaxy Nutritional Foods.

Makes 4 servings

2   large baking potatoes

1   cup broccoli florets

2   tsps olive oil

½   cup Great Northern beans (drained and rinsed if using canned, or cooked and rinsed if using dried)

½   tsp salt

   freshly ground pepper to taste

¼–⅓ cup shredded vegan cheese (soy-free and nut-free)

Preheat oven to 350°F.

Wash and pierce whole potatoes. Bake potatoes for about 1 hour. Potatoes are done when a fork easily pierces them.

While potatoes are cooking, blanch broccoli in boiling water for 10 seconds; then rinse under cold water. Set aside.

Cut potatoes in half lengthwise. When potatoes are cool enough to handle, scoop out flesh. leaving a ¼-inch border.

Mash potato with olive oil, beans, salt, and pepper. Mix broccoli into potato mixture. Spoon mashed potatoes into potato shells, and top with cheese.

Increase oven temperature to 375°F. Bake for 5–10 more minutes or until cheese melts.

Per serving: 225 calories, 4 g fat, 43 g carbohydrates, 4 g fiber, 7 g protein

Stuffed Baked Potatoes

Served with a bowl of Throw-Together Tomato Soup (page 59), these stuffed potatoes make a warm and comforting dinner.

Makes 4 servings

2   *large baking potatoes*

2   *tsps olive oil*

½   *cup Great Northern beans (drained and rinsed if from a can, or cooked and rinsed if using dried beans)*

½   *tsp salt*

  freshly ground pepper to taste

  sprinkling of paprika

Preheat oven to 350°F.

Wash and pierce whole potatoes. Bake potatoes for about 1 hour. Potatoes are done when a fork easily pierces them.

Cut potatoes in half lengthwise. When potatoes are cool enough to handle, scoop out flesh, leaving a ¼-inch border.

Mash potato with olive oil, beans, salt, and pepper. Spoon mashed potatoes into potato shells and top with a sprinkling of paprika.

Bake for 15 more minutes or until the potatoes form a golden crust.

Per serving: 141 calories, 2 g fat, 26 g carbohydrates, 3 g fiber, 5 g protein

Pierogi

Spring roll wrappers made from rice (make sure they're just rice and water, with no egg or other allergenic ingredients) make the perfect wrapper for this dish. Serve these traditional Polish dumplings with Ruby Coleslaw (page 44) for an interesting mix of colors and textures.

Makes 12 pierogi

6	medium baking potatoes		freshly ground black pepper
1	medium onion	12	spring roll wrappers
3	tbsps olive oil, divided		
1	tsp salt		

Peel and chop potatoes. Put chopped potatoes into a medium saucepan and cover with water. Bring to a boil, reduce heat to a high simmer, and cook until potatoes are tender. While potatoes are cooking, finely chop onion. Heat 1 tablespoon olive oil over medium-high heat. Add onion and cook until tender, but not browned. Set aside.

Remove potatoes from water with a slotted spoon. Mash thoroughly in a large bowl. Add salt, pepper, and cooked onion. Mix thoroughly.

Add warm water to a flat-bottomed bowl. Dip one spring roll wrapper at a time, dipping one side and then the other. Shake off excess water. Lay 1 wrapper on a dinner plate. Scoop ¼ cup of potato mixture onto one side of the wrapper. Roll the pierogi burrito-style, tucking the sides in as you roll the mixture in the wrapper.

Heat remaining olive oil in a large skillet. Cook pierogi in batches small enough so they do not touch in the pan. Turn pierogi to be sure that they are cooked on all sides. Remove pierogi to a paper-towel-lined plate to drain off excess oil.

Per serving: 143 calories, 4 g fat, 25 g carbohydrates, 2 g fiber, 3 g protein

Nana's Latkes

My boys love to eat potato pancakes at my mother's house. She likes to prepare them early in the day and then reheat them on brown-paper-lined cookie sheets to re-crisp them. Serve the latkes with applesauce or plain coconut-based yogurt.

Makes 10 potato pancakes

8	baking potatoes
1	onion
1	tsp salt
	fresh ground pepper
2	tbsps flaxseed meal
3	tbsps water
¼	cup gluten-free flour
1	tbsp canola oil

Peel and grate potatoes and onion. Squeeze dry with a clean dishtowel (or two).

Toss potatoes and onion together; add salt and pepper.

In a small bowl, combine flaxseed meal with water. Let sit for 1 minute. Add gluten-free flour and flaxseed mixture to potatoes and mix well.

Heat canola oil in skillet.

Form palm-sized pancakes with your hands.

Cook over medium-high heat until browned on both sides (about 3 minutes per side). Drain on paper-towel-lined plate or cookie sheet.

Per serving: 167 calories, 2 g fat, 34 g carbohydrates, 3 g fiber, 4 g protein

Fajitas

Serve these fajitas with Refried Beans (page 128), Chipotle Guacamole (page 22), H&J Creamy Chipotle Sauce (page 100), and warmed corn tortillas.

Makes 4 servings

1   tbsp lime juice

2   tbsps olive oil

2   garlic cloves, minced

¼   tsp salt

1   onion, sliced

1   green pepper, sliced

1   portabella mushroom, sliced

1   bunch broccoli, divided into florets

1   jalapeño, diced

In a large bowl, thoroughly combine lime juice, olive oil, garlic, and salt.

Add onion, green pepper, mushroom, broccoli, and jalapeño to the marinade. Let vegetables marinate for 15 to 30 minutes, stirring occasionally.

Pour all the ingredients into a large skillet or sauté pan.

Cook on high heat until vegetables are tender but still retain some crispness.

Lunches & Dinners

Per serving: 91 calories, 7 g fat, 7 g carbohydrates, 1 g fiber, 2 g protein

H&J Creamy Chipotle Sauce

This sauce is based on a delicious sauce created by my great friends, Heather and John. Serve this creamy, zingy topping with fajitas, roasted potatoes, or steamed vegetables.

Makes ⅞ cup

1   6-ounce container plain coconut-based yogurt

1½   chipotle peppers in adobo sauce

1   clove garlic

2   tbsps orange juice

Combine all ingredients in a blender or food processor. Blend until smooth.

Warm in a small saucepan over medium-low heat.

Per ⅛ cup serving: 27 calories, 3 g fat, 3 g carbohydrates, 1 g fiber, 2 g protein

Jerk Portabella Mushroom

This mushroom dish pairs well with Quinoa Pilaf (page 136) and packs quite a spicy kick. To cool off warmed-up taste buds, serve up some refreshing Coconut Sorbet (page 218).

Makes one mushroom

½   tsp allspice
¼   tsp cayenne
½   tsp thyme
1   garlic clove, minced
1   tsp brown sugar
2   tsps lemon juice
1   tbsp olive oil
1   portabella mushroom cap

In a flat bowl, combine all ingredients but the mushroom.

Remove the stem and gills of the mushroom. Using a fork, score top and bottom of the mushroom several times. Press both sides of mushroom down into spice mixture. Spoon any remaining seasoning on both sides.

Cook mushroom over high heat in a dry skillet (or on a grill) for 2–3 minutes per side, or until the mushroom is tender.

Per mushroom: 165 calories, 14 g fat, 110 g carbohydrates, 2 g fiber, 2 g protein

Corn Cakes with Roasted Tomatoes and Onions

Savory corn cakes pair really nicely with Roasted Tomatoes and Onions (page 103). You can also top corn cakes with salsa or sliced avocado. My kids eat them with maple syrup.

Makes 8 servings

1½ cups cornmeal

½ tsp baking soda

¼ tsp salt

2 tbsps flaxseed meal

¼ cup water

1½ cups Creamy Corn Soup (page 62)

1 tsp olive oil

1 recipe Roasted Tomatoes and Onions (page 103)

In a medium bowl, combine cornmeal, baking soda, and salt.

In a small bowl, combine flaxseed meal and water; let sit for a minute or two. Mix flaxseed slurry and soup into cornmeal.

Brush a skillet with olive oil. Heat skillet over medium-high heat until a drop of water dances when dropped onto the pan.

Drop a ¼-cup scoop of batter onto the hot pan. Cover with a lid, and cook for about 2 minutes. Turn and cook corn cake on the other side.

Serve corn cakes with Roasted Tomatoes and Onions.

Per serving: 150 calories, 2 g fat, 29 g carbohydrates, 2 g fiber, 3 g protein

Roasted Tomatoes and Onions

Makes 2 cups

4	tomatoes
1	red onion
2	tbsps olive oil
½	tsp salt
	freshly ground black pepper
2	tbsps fresh cilantro

Preheat oven to 400°F.

Remove cores and seeds from tomatoes. Chop into thick chunks.

Thickly slice onion.

Toss tomatoes and onions with olive oil, salt, and pepper.

Roast for 18–20 minutes.

Toss with chopped cilantro.

Per ½ cup serving: 111 calories, 6 g fat, 12 g carbohydrates, 2 g fiber, 2 g protein

Pot Pie

One of the great pleasures of fall is serving up a delicious pot pie. This version uses chickpeas as the protein source, but any bean will work.

Makes 8 servings

2	tbsps olive oil	1	tbsp nutritional yeast
2	baking potatoes, peeled and chopped	1	tbsp garlic pepper
2	carrots, peeled and sliced	1	tbsp poultry seasoning
1	onion, chopped	1	tsp dried dill, or 1 tbsp fresh dill
1	small head of broccoli florets	1	tbsp cornstarch mixed with 2 tbsps cold water
6	mushrooms, button or cremini, chopped	1	15-ounce can chickpeas, drained and rinsed
1½	cups vegetable broth or water	1	recipe gluten-free biscuit batter, not baked (page 160)

Preheat oven to 425°F.

Heat olive oil over medium-high heat. Add potatoes, carrots, onion, and broccoli. Sauté for 3–5 minutes, until slightly soft. Add mushrooms; sauté 1 more minute.

In a medium bowl, mix together broth, nutritional yeast, garlic pepper, poultry seasoning, and dill. Mix in diluted cornstarch.

Toss vegetables and drained chickpeas with sauce. Pour into 2- or 3-quart baking dish. Top vegetables with biscuit batter.

Bake 25 to 30 minutes.

Per serving: 311 calories, 12 g fat, 47 g carbohydrates, 6 g fiber, 8 g protein

Creamy Polenta

Polenta, or cornmeal mush, can act as a creamy alternative to rice or pasta. You can also spread warm polenta in an oiled pan, refrigerate until firm, slice it, and fry or broil the slices. This treatment will give your polenta a firmer texture. Polenta is good for any time of day. It makes a comforting breakfast and is an awesome base for sauces and stews. Experiment with different polenta textures and different herb mix-ins.

Makes 4 servings (½ cup each)

1½ cups rice milk

1½ cups water

1   tbsp olive oil

1   cup coarse cornmeal

   salt & pepper to taste

In a medium saucepan, combine rice milk, water, and olive oil. Bring to a boil.

Whisk in cornmeal and salt and pepper.

Cook over medium heat, stirring frequently, until polenta pulls away from the sides of the pot.

Per serving: 185 calories, 5 g fat, 32 g carbohydrates, 2 g fiber, 3 g protein

Vegetable Polenta

This is a good example of how a stew can be paired with polenta to make a delicious, filling entrée. Use this vegetable stew as a starting point, but you can experiment with any stew. Italian- and Mexican-influenced stews are an especially nice fit with polenta.

Makes 8 servings

2	recipes (8 servings) Creamy Polenta (page 105)
6	sun-dried tomato halves
1	tbsp olive oil
3	garlic cloves, minced
½	onion, chopped
1	green bell pepper, chopped
1	bunch broccoli florets, chopped
1	15-ounce can garbanzo beans, drained and rinsed
1	28-ounce can fire-roasted diced tomatoes, drained

Prepare polenta according to directions.

Cover sun-dried tomatoes with boiling water. Let sit 10 minutes, or until tender.

Heat olive oil in a large skillet or sauté pan. Over medium-high heat, cook garlic, onion, and green pepper for 2–3 minutes, or until flavorful and beginning to soften.

Remove sun-dried tomato halves from water and slice.

Add tomatoes and broccoli florets to pan. Cook for 5 minutes or until broccoli is tender, not mushy. Add beans and fire-roasted tomatoes and heat through, about 3 more minutes.

Spoon stew over polenta.

Per serving: 307 calories, 8 g fat, 54 g carbohydrates, 7 g fiber, 5 g protein

PIZZA

Pizza is a constant on our family's menu. We make pizzas with this crust or individual pizzas on sliced biscuits, toast, or corn tortillas. Casey always eats his lunch when it's pizza!

Polenta Pizza Crust

Makes 6 servings

4	cups vegetable broth
¼	tsp salt
2	cups cornmeal
2	tsps olive oil, divided

Preheat oven to 425°F.

Bring vegetable broth and salt to a boil. Slowly whisk in cornmeal. Continue stirring until very thick and smooth.

Brush a 6-inch by 12-inch baking sheet with 1 teaspoon olive oil. Spread polenta over baking sheet, and brush with remaining olive oil.

Bake 25–30 minutes (or longer for crispier crust).

Per serving: 205 calories, 1 g fat, 44 g carbohydrates, 2 g fiber, 4 g protein

No-Cook Pizza Sauce

Any leftover pasta sauce can be transformed into pizza sauce. Experiment with chunky sauces, smooth sauces, or pesto. If you don't have any leftover sauce, you can make this pizza sauce in practically no time at all.

Makes 2 cups

1	28-ounce can diced tomatoes
1	tsp dried basil
1	tsp dried oregano
½	tsp dried thyme
¼	tsp salt
¼	tsp red pepper flakes
1	tbsp olive oil
1	tsp granulated sugar
1	garlic clove, minced
	freshly ground pepper to taste

Combine all ingredients in a food processor or blender. Blend until smooth.

Per ½ cup serving: 73 calories, 4 g fat, 9 g carbohydrates, 2 g fiber, 2 g protein

Pizzeria-Style Pizza

If you prefer a cheese-less pizza, you can omit the cheese.

Makes 6 servings

1   cup No-Cook Pizza
     Sauce (page 108)

1   Polenta Pizza Crust
     (page 107)

½   green pepper, sliced

6   white mushrooms,
     sliced

½   onion, sliced

10   pitted black olives,
     sliced

6   ounces soy- and
     nut-free vegan cheese
     (optional)

Preheat oven to 425°F.

Spread sauce over baked crust. Distribute vegetables over sauce. Top with cheese, if using.

Bake 12–15 minutes, or until cheese is melted and vegetables are tender yet still retain some crispness.

Per serving: 280 calories, 6 g fat, 51 g carbohydrates, 3 g fiber, 6 g protein

Spinach Pizza

Lush and flavorful, creamed spinach makes a terrific base for a cheese-free pizza.

Makes 6 servings

1	*Polenta Pizza Crust (page 107)*	Bake pizza crust according to the recipe.
2	*recipes (1½ cups) Creamed Spinach (page 138)*	Top with spinach, and bake an additional 10 minutes at 425°F.
3	*roma tomatoes*	Remove core and seeds from tomatoes. Slice tomatoes and basil.
1	*tbsp sliced fresh basil*	Top cooked pizza with tomatoes and basil.

Per serving: 287 calories, 7 g fat, 52 g carbohydrates, 2 g fiber, 2 g protein

PASTA OPTIONS

There is such an abundance of choices when you start thinking about pasta and pasta-like dishes for your welcoming kitchen. You can make beautiful, delicious "noodles" by peeling vegetables like carrots or zucchini into ribbons. You can buy high-quality, gluten-free, dried pastas made out of brown rice, corn, or quinoa at grocery stores or online. You can serve your favorite pasta sauces over polenta, gnocchi, or spaghetti squash. With so many exciting possibilities, you might find yourself wishing it was pasta night every night!

Creamy Pasta Sauce

Pureed roasted cauliflower and garlic provide the creaminess in this delicious interpretation of a tomato cream sauce.

Makes 6 servings

1	medium head cauliflower
6	cloves of garlic
2	tbsps olive oil
3	cups pasta sauce, either bottled sauce or Easy Tomato Basil Sauce (page 117)

Preheat oven to 450°F.

Cut cauliflower florets from head. Remove papery skin from garlic, but leave cloves whole. Toss cauliflower and garlic with olive oil. Spread on a cookie sheet. Bake 5–10 minutes, until cauliflower is tender, but not burned.

Puree vegetables and pasta sauce in food processor or blender. Pour into saucepan and heat through.

Serve with the wheat-free pasta of your choosing.

Per ½ cup: 154 calories, 6 g fat, 22 g carbohydrates, 5 g fiber, 4 g protein

Pasta with Greens and Beans

Make sure you thoroughly wash greens before using since they can hold onto a lot of dirt and grit.

Makes 4 servings

1	bunch chard
1	bunch spinach
1	garlic clove
1	tbsp olive oil
1	tsp dried oregano
2	tbsps lemon juice
½	cup vegan white wine
1	15-ounce can garbanzo beans, drained and rinsed
1	15-ounce can quartered artichoke hearts, drained and rinsed
½	tsp red pepper flakes (optional)
1	pound gluten-free fusilli or other chunky pasta

Thoroughly wash and drain chard and spinach. Chop greens.

Sauté garlic in olive oil. Add chard and spinach. Add oregano, lemon juice, wine, beans, artichoke hearts, and red pepper flakes. Sauté until greens are wilted.

Cook pasta according to package directions.

Combine pasta and sauce.

Per serving: 433 calories, 12 g fat, 69 g carbohydrates, 13 g fiber, 12 g protein

Basil Pesto

Bold flavors really round out dishes that use nontraditional ingredients. You can add a dollop of pesto to brighten up a soup or spice up a sandwich. You can also experiment with different herbs. For example, cilantro pesto can provide an interesting kick to rice-based dishes. If you're not going to use all the pesto, you can freeze portions in an ice-cube tray and then transfer the frozen pesto cubes to a freezer-safe container.

Makes ⅔ cups

2	*ounces fresh basil*
2	*tbsps olive oil*
2	*cloves garlic*
2	*tbsps chopped pumpkin seeds*
1	*tbsp nutritional yeast*
	salt & pepper to taste

Finely chop all ingredients in food processor.

Per ⅔ cups: 488 calories, 41 g fat, 16 g carbohydrates, 8 g fiber, 24 g protein

Pesto Pasta Salad

This pasta can be served warm or cold. You can replace the artichoke hearts with fresh produce—blanched broccoli or asparagus, for example.

Makes 4 servings

1   *pound gluten-free pasta*

6   *sun-dried tomato halves*

2   *plum tomatoes, chopped*

6–7 *artichoke hearts, chopped*

1   *15-ounce can garbanzo beans, drained and rinsed*

½   *recipe Basil Pesto (⅓ cup) (page 114)*

2   *tbsps olive oil*

salt & pepper

Cook pasta according to package directions, drain, and rinse.

Soak sun-dried tomatoes in boiling water to cover until soft (about 10 minutes). Drain and chop sun-dried tomatoes.

Combine pasta, sun-dried tomatoes, plum tomatoes, artichoke hearts, and garbanzo beans.

Toss with pesto and olive oil. Season with salt and pepper to taste.

Per serving: 669 calories, 16 g fat, 113 g carbohydrates, 7 g fiber, 19 g protein

Gnocchi

I love these Italian potato-based dumplings. Serve them with your favorite pasta sauce.

Makes 6 servings

5	*medium baking potatoes*
1½	*cups gluten-free flour*
1	*tsp salt*
1	*tsp pepper*

Peel and chop potatoes. Place potatoes in a large saucepan or stockpot. Cover with water. Boil until soft. Remove potatoes from water and place in a large bowl. Mash potatoes until smooth.

Add flour, salt, and pepper. Mix well. (It might be easiest to use your hands.)

Bring water to a boil in a large saucepan or stockpot.

While water is heating, roll dough into four balls.

Working with one ball at a time, dust work board with gluten-free flour; then roll ball into a ¾-inch-thick rope. Slice rope into 1-inch pieces.

Working in batches, drop gnocchi into boiling water. Gnocchi are ready when they float to the surface, about 2 minutes. Remove gnocchi from water with a slotted spoon.

Per serving: 128 calories, 1 g fat, 28 g carbohydrates, 3 g fiber, 4 g protein

Easy Tomato Basil Sauce

I like to make a double batch of this versatile sauce and freeze half. That way, I can boil up some pasta and have a home-cooked meal in no time.

Makes 3½ cups

2   tbsps olive oil

3   cloves garlic, minced

5   cups diced tomatoes, or 2 28-ounce cans diced tomatoes, drained

1   6-ounce can tomato paste

1   tsp sugar

½   cup vegan red wine

2   tbsps fresh basil, chopped

2   tsps dried oregano

freshly ground pepper to taste

In a large saucepan or stockpot, heat olive oil over medium heat. Add garlic; sauté for 2 minutes until fragrant. Add remaining ingredients and stir thoroughly.

Simmer uncovered 1 to 1½ hours.

Per ½ cup serving: 97 calories, 4 g fat, 11 g carbohydrates, 3 g fiber, 2 g protein

Pasta Pot

What could be better than dinner in just over half an hour? This one-pot meal is very versatile; you can use any vegetables you have on hand. Asparagus, broccoli, or mushrooms are excellent options.

Makes 8 servings

2	*tbsps olive oil*
½	*large eggplant, thinly sliced*
1	*cup pitted black olives*
1	*cup grated zucchini*
1	*25-ounce jar pasta sauce*
½	*cup vegan red wine*
3	*cups water*
12	*ounces gluten-free pasta*

In a large pot, heat olive oil over medium-high heat. Add eggplant. Cook 5 minutes.

Add olives and zucchini.

Cook 5 minutes more.

Add sauce, wine, water, and pasta.

Cover and cook 18–20 minutes or until pasta is tender.

Per serving: 300 calories, 8 g fat, 47 g carbohydrates, 4 g fiber, 6 g protein

Thai-Inspired Rice Noodles

You can use other vegetables in addition to the broccoli or in place of it. Experiment with julienned carrots, bean sprouts, or pea pods. Ume plum vinegar is an ingredient used in Asian cooking. If you don't have it, you can leave it out.

Makes 8 servings

1   cup Sunflower Seed Butter (store-bought or use recipe on page 14)

1   cup vegetable broth (store-bought or use recipe on page 60)

1   tbsp lime juice

2   cloves garlic, minced

2   tbsps rice vinegar

1   tbsp fresh ginger, minced

⅛   tsp hot pepper sauce (optional)

12   ounces Thai rice noodles

2   cups steamed broccoli florets

Combine sunflower seed butter, broth, lime juice, garlic, vinegar, ginger, and hot pepper sauce in a blender or food processor. Blend until smooth.

Cook rice noodles according to package directions.

Toss noodles with sauce and broccoli.

DIPPING SAUCE VARIATION

Follow directions for sauce above. Serve at room temperature with a variety of raw vegetables for dipping.

Per serving: 350 calories, 16 g fat, 46 g carbohydrates, 1 g fiber, 8 g protein

Kasha Varnishkas (Pasta with Kasha)

This traditional Eastern European dish is hearty and filling. Serve it with a crisp green salad or Herbed Broccoli Salad (page 50).

Makes 8 servings

12 ounces gluten-free chunky pasta (like rotini or penne)

2 cups vegetable broth

¼ cup olive oil, divided

1 cup dried kasha (roasted buckwheat)

1 onion, finely chopped

1 cup thinly sliced mushrooms

Cook pasta according to directions.

Bring vegetable broth and 2 tablespoons olive oil to a boil. Add kasha, cover, and reduce heat to simmer. Cook kasha for 10 minutes or until liquid is absorbed.

Heat 1 tablespoon olive oil in a skillet. Add onion and mushrooms. Cook until soft and mushrooms have released their liquid.

Drain pasta and toss with remaining tablespoon of olive oil.

In a large bowl, toss pasta, kasha, and vegetables to combine.

Per serving: 310 calories, 8 g fat, 52 g carbohydrates, 1 g fiber, 7 g protein

Awesome Artichoke Sauce

This sauce is so easy, it's hard to believe that it's also special-occasion ready, but it is! Serve this sauce over gluten-free pasta and pass some Karma-zan (page 125).

Makes 2 servings

3	*garlic cloves*
1	*15-ounce can artichoke hearts, rinsed, or frozen artichoke hearts, thawed*
¼	*cup olive oil*
¼	*cup vegan white wine*
1	*tbsp lemon juice*
1	*tbsp plus 1 tsp sliced fresh basil*
	freshly ground black pepper

Finely chop garlic.

Roughly chop artichoke hearts.

Heat olive oil in a large skillet over medium-high heat.

Add garlic and sauté until soft, but not brown.

Add wine, lemon juice, and artichoke hearts; sauté for 3 minutes.

Add basil and pepper; stir to combine, and sauté for another minute or two.

Per serving: 320 calories, 28 fat, 13 g carbohydrates, 5 g fiber, 4 g protein

Roasted Tomato Sauce

Although nothing could be easier than putting this pasta sauce together, it couldn't be more delicious! It's great for unexpected company, since it comes together in less than half an hour.

Makes 4 servings

4	tomatoes
6	cloves of garlic
2	tbsps olive oil
¼	tsp salt
	freshly ground black pepper
2	tbsps fresh basil

Preheat oven to 400°F.

Remove cores and seeds from tomatoes. Cut tomatoes into wedges.

Smash garlic cloves with the side of a large knife's blade.

Toss tomato wedges and garlic with olive oil and salt and pepper on a baking sheet.

Cook 20–25 minutes, checking to make sure that the mixture doesn't burn.

Blend vegetables in a food processor or blender.

Slice basil into ribbons. Top pasta sauce with basil.

Per serving: 89 calories, 7 fat, 6 g carbohydrates, 2 g fiber, 1 g protein

Spaghetti Squash with Herbed Garlic Oil

This is just one way to prepare spaghetti squash. You can use this as a pasta alternative with any of the sauces included in this book.

Makes 6 one-cup servings

1	*medium spaghetti squash*
2	*tbsps Herbed Garlic Oil (page 124)*
¼	*cup Karma-zan "Cheese" Topping (page 125)*
	freshly ground pepper to taste

Preheat oven to 350°F.

Pierce squash with a fork in several places. Bake 1½ hours or until squash is easily pierced with a fork. Cut in half and remove seeds. Scrape flesh with the tines of a fork to form spaghetti-like threads.

Toss squash with garlic oil, Karma-zan topping, and pepper.

Lunches & Dinners

Per serving: 109 calories, 7 g fat, 12 g carbohydrates, 1 g fiber, 2 g protein

Herbed Garlic Oil

This oil is delicious brushed on corn on the cob, drizzled over baked potatoes, or tossed with hot rice or quinoa. Experiment with different herbs like dill or rosemary.

Makes 2 tablespoons

2	*garlic cloves*
2	*tbsps olive oil*
1	*tsp finely chopped cilantro*

Smash garlic with the side of a knife. Pour olive oil in a small bowl or coffee cup and add garlic.

Heat in a microwave oven on high for 30 seconds or in a small saucepan on the stove until oil is heated, but not boiling.

Remove garlic. Stir in cilantro.

Per 1 tbsp serving: 124 calories, 14 g fat, 1 g carbohydrates, 0 g fiber, 0 g protein

Karma-zan "Cheese" Topping

This faux parmesan cheese makes a great topping for pasta, salad, and soup. If you don't have an extra biscuit, a piece of gluten-free toast works just as well.

Makes 1 cup

1	biscuit (page 160)
⅜	tsp nutritional yeast
⅛	tsp garlic powder
⅛	tsp salt

Use a slightly stale biscuit, or toast the biscuit to dry it out a little.

Combine all ingredients in a food processor and pulse until thoroughly combined.

Per serving: 151 calories, 7 g fat, 20 g carbohydrates, 3 g fiber, 3 g protein

Garden-Fresh Herb Pasta

This flavorful pasta works equally well as a hot entrée or a pasta salad served at room temperature. If you have an indoor herb garden, you can enjoy a taste of summer all year.

Makes 4 servings

1	pound chunky gluten-free pasta (for example, fusilli)
½	cup fresh basil leaves
½	cup fresh cilantro leaves
½	cup fresh parsley
1	cup fresh spinach leaves
1	cup Great Northern beans
2	cloves garlic
¼	tsp salt
2	tbsps lemon juice
¼	cup olive oil
	freshly ground pepper to taste
3	plum tomatoes, chopped

Cook pasta according to package directions.

In a food processor, combine remaining ingredients except for tomatoes.

When pasta is cooked, drain in a colander and then return to the pot.

Toss hot pasta with sauce. Toss in tomatoes.

Per serving: 353 calories, 15 g fat, 49 g carbohydrates, 10 g fiber, 9 g protein

SIDEKICKS

Although entrees get all the credit for a great meal, it is often the side dishes that most warm our hearts. When I've had a tough day, mashed potatoes can ease the pain. (I must admit that I sometimes look forward to evenings when my husband is out playing with his band, because I can make a dinner of just mashed potatoes and dessert for myself!) If you want to shake up your next dinner party and give your guests a thrill, try putting out a buffet of side dishes and let everyone make up their own menu.

Refried Beans

These beans are extremely versatile. You can serve them on their own with chips or tortillas for dipping, or you can use them as a component of other recipes, like Mexican Lasagna (page 81).

Makes 4 servings

½ onion, chopped

2 cloves garlic, minced

1 tbsp olive oil

1 tsp cumin

1 15-ounce can pinto beans, drained but not rinsed

Sauté onion and garlic in oil until soft, 3 to 5 minutes.

Add cumin; cook 1 minute more.

Add beans and heat through.

Mash bean mixture with a potato masher or fork.

Per ½ cup serving: 130 calories, 4 fat, 18 g carbohydrates, 5 g fiber, 5 g protein

Fried Green Tomatoes

Although my husband has been known to eat a whole batch of these tomatoes all on their own, you might want to serve them with a salad or a cup of soup for a really tasty lunch.

Makes 4 servings

Lunches & Dinners

4   medium or 3 large green tomatoes

¼   cup cornmeal

¼   tsp salt

    freshly ground black pepper to taste

¼   cup rice milk

2   tbsps canola oil

Slice tomatoes and set aside.

In a shallow bowl, combine cornmeal, salt, and pepper.

Pour rice milk into a separate bowl.

Heat canola oil in a medium skillet.

Dip tomato slices, one at a time, in the rice milk, then the cornmeal, making sure to coat both sides.

Cook tomatoes in the hot oil, about 2 minutes per side. You'll know it's time to flip the tomatoes when the tops begin to look moist.

Remove golden tomatoes to a paper-towel-lined plate to absorb excess oil.

Per serving: 134 calories, 8 fat, 16 g carbohydrates, 2 g fiber, 2 g protein

Homestyle Stuffing

Serve this delicious, traditional-style stuffing alongside Rosemary Portabella Mushrooms (page 134) and Maple Sweet Potatoes (page 137) for a Thanksgiving-worthy dinner. Don't forget to finish with a slice of Pumpkin Pie (page 195).

Makes 6 servings

8	slices gluten-free bread (such as tapioca loaf or brown rice loaf)
2	tbsps olive oil
2	carrots, coarsely chopped
1	onion, finely chopped
1	cup chopped mushrooms (button or cremini)
¼	tsp black pepper
½	tsp poultry seasoning
2	cups vegetable broth

Preheat oven to 200°F.

Toast bread in oven for 10–15 minutes or until fairly dried; chop into ½-inch pieces.

Increase oven temperature to 350°F. Oil a 2-quart casserole.

Sauté carrots, onion, and mushrooms in olive oil for 2–3 minutes, until slightly soft.

Add black pepper and poultry seasoning; sauté for another couple of minutes. Add bread and toss to mix. Add broth and toss to mix.

Spread mixture in casserole. Bake for 35–45 minutes (use longer cooking time to make a drier stuffing).

Per serving: 121 calories, 5 fat, 18 g carbohydrates, 2 g fiber, 2 g protein

Dill Carrots

Both sweet and a little salty, these herby carrots are a colorful accompaniment to Veggie Loaf (page 85).

Makes 4 servings

1	tbsp olive oil
3	carrots, peeled and thinly sliced
2	tbsps agave nectar
½	tsp salt
2	tbsps fresh chopped dill

Heat olive oil in a medium skillet.

Add carrots and cook until tender, but still firm, not mushy.

Add agave nectar, salt, and dill and cook for another minute to combine flavors.

Per serving: 82 calories, 4 g fat, 13 g carbohydrates, 2 g fiber, 1 g protein

Old-Fashioned Mashed Potatoes

Serve these deliciously creamy mashed potatoes with Jerk Portabella Mushroom (page 101) and Summertime Corn Salad (page 49).

Makes 6 servings

6	*medium red potatoes (or other baking potato)*
½	*cup rice milk*
2	*tsp olive oil*
½	*tsp salt*

Peel and chop potatoes. In a medium saucepan, cover potatoes with water. Bring to a boil, reduce heat, and simmer until potatoes are fork-tender. Drain potatoes and transfer to a bowl.

Add rice milk, olive oil, and salt.

Mash all ingredients together with a potato masher or fork.

Per serving: 170 calories, 2 g fat, 38 g carbohydrates, 5 g fiber, 4 g protein

Oven-Baked Wedge Fries

Burgers and fries are just the beginning of how you can serve these easy, flavorful potatoes. Try serving them alongside Chipotle Guacamole (page 22) or Sesame-Free Hummus (page 27) for a filling snack or light lunch.

Makes 4 servings

2	*large or 3 medium red potatoes*
2	*tsp olive oil*
½	*tsp seasoned salt*

Preheat oven to 450°F.

Wash potatoes and cut them in half.
Slice potatoes into ½-inch-thick wedges.

Coat a small cookie sheet with olive oil.
Lay potato slices on oiled sheet.
Turn potato slices to coat on both sides.
Sprinkle potato slices with seasoned salt.

Bake until light brown, 15–20 minutes.

Per serving: 125 calories, 1 g fat, 25 g carbohydrates, 2 g fiber, 3 g protein

Rosemary Portabella Mushrooms

These savory mushrooms round out a special meal when paired with Spinach and Cherry Tomato Risotto (page 87).

Makes 4 servings

3   medium or 4 small portabella mushroom caps

¼   cup olive oil

2   tbsps balsamic vinegar

1½   tsps fresh rosemary, chopped

2   garlic cloves, minced

¼   tsp salt

Wipe portabella mushrooms clean with a damp cloth or use a mushroom brush.

In a shallow bowl, make a marinade out of the remaining ingredients.

Marinate mushrooms for an hour, periodically spooning marinade over mushrooms.

Slice mushrooms into thick (1-inch) slices. Combine mushroom slices and marinade in a large skillet.

Cook on high heat for five minutes, tossing regularly to ensure even cooking.

Per serving: 151 calories, 14 g fat, 6 g carbohydrates, 1 g fiber, 2 g protein

Dill Rice

Enjoy this rice for a change-of-pace lunch instead of a sandwich or salad.

Makes 4 servings

2	cups water
2	tbsps olive oil
¼	tsp salt
1	cup long-grain brown rice
½	cup frozen lima beans
2	tbsps fresh dill

In a small saucepan, bring water, olive oil, and salt to a boil. Add rice to boiling water, cover, and reduce heat to a simmer.

Cook for 30 minutes, or until rice is mostly cooked, but still al dente.

Add lima beans and dill to hot rice, cover, and return to low heat for 10 minutes.

Fluff with a fork before serving.

Per serving: 258 calories, 8 g fat, 41 g carbohydrates, 3 g fiber, 5 g protein

Quinoa Pilaf

You can play with this tasty, basic pilaf to come up with lots of different side dishes. Try adding dried fruit and toasted pumpkin seeds or artichoke hearts and sun-dried tomatoes for a delicious alternative. Since quinoa is higher in protein than other grains, you can use this pilaf to round out a meal that features vegetables in a central role.

Makes 6 serving

2	*cups vegetable broth*
1	*cup quinoa*
1	*tbsp olive oil*
¼	*cup chopped onion*
5	*white mushrooms, sliced (about 1 cup)*

In a small saucepan, bring vegetable broth to a boil.

Thoroughly rinse quinoa, and add to broth. Reduce heat, cover, and simmer 15 minutes.

In a large skillet, heat olive oil over medium heat. Add onion and mushrooms and sauté until soft.

Stir quinoa into vegetables.

Per serving: 134 calories, 4 g fat, 20 g carbohydrates, 2 g fiber, 5 g protein

Maple Sweet Potatoes

Another great way to enjoy sweet potatoes or white potatoes is to bake them and serve them with olive oil and salt. This is also a good thing to remember if you are stumped about what you can order at a restaurant. Lots of restaurants can easily serve you a plain baked potato or sweet potato with some olive oil for drizzling; add a salad to that and you have a filling (and safe) meal to order.

Makes 4 servings

2   *sweet potatoes*

¼   *tsp salt*

¼   *cup maple syrup*

       canola oil spray

Preheat oven to 375°F.

Peel sweet potatoes and cut in thick slices.

Lightly oil a baking dish. Place sweet potato slices in dish, sprinkle with salt, and drizzle with maple syrup.

Bake for 25 to 35 minutes, or until sweet potatoes are tender with slightly crispy edges.

Per serving: 110 calories, 0 g fat, 27 g carbohydrates, 2 g fiber, 1 g protein

Creamed Spinach

This is a very versatile side dish. As a topping for a baked potato, it makes a delicious lunch, but you can also use creamed spinach as a flavorful component of a complete dinner. Serve it alongside Jerk Portabella Mushrooms and Quinoa Pilaf for an interesting meal.

Makes ¾ cup

1   bunch spinach, washed and stems removed, but not dried

1   piece gluten-free bread—such as toast, ½ hamburger roll, biscuit (page 160)

2   tbsps olive oil

1   clove garlic, minced

½   tsp salt

     freshly ground black pepper to taste

2–4 tbsps rice milk

Roughly chop spinach. Wilt spinach in a dry skillet.

Cut bread into 2-inch pieces and briefly soak in water.

Combine wilted spinach with bread in food processor, fitted with steel blade. Process until finely chopped.

Heat olive oil over medium heat. Sauté garlic until fragrant. Add salt and pepper. Add 2 tablespoons rice milk. Add spinach mixture.

Add more rice milk until mixture reaches desired consistency. Heat through.

Per ¼ cup serving: 153 calories, 11 g fat, 13 g carbohydrates, 3 g fiber, 4 g protein

Root Vegetable Chips

Even though I don't particularly love beets, I can't stop eating beet chips! This recipe is a great way to cook late-fall root vegetables that are bountiful when summer produce is becoming a memory. This recipe uses beets, but you can follow the same technique with other root vegetables, like turnips or rutabagas.

Makes 4 servings

1   large beet or 2 small

1   tbsp olive oil

⅛   tsp salt

Preheat oven to 425°F.

Peel and thinly slice beet. Toss with olive oil and salt. Spread slices on a cookie sheet.

Bake for 10 minutes, flip to other side, and cook 5 to 7 minutes.

Per serving: 47 calories, 3 g fat, 4 g carbohydrates, 1 g fiber, 1 g protein

Sweet and Savory Winter Squash

We eat a lot of winter squash in the cold months. We get a box of seasonal produce every week from a Community Supported Agriculture (CSA) farm we belong to. Our CSA boxes in the fall and winter come filled with acorn, butternut, and kombucha squashes. We often eat them cooked with olive oil and brown sugar, but sometimes we want something a little out of the ordinary. This recipe makes a colorful side dish at Thanksgiving feasts.

Makes 4 servings

2	tbsps orange juice
1	tbsp olive oil
½	tsp cumin
¼	tsp cinnamon
⅛	tsp chili powder
¼	tsp salt
5–6	cups peeled and cubed (about 1-inch cubes) winter squash

Preheat oven to 425°F.

In a large bowl, combine orange juice, olive oil, and seasonings. Add squash cubes; toss to coat. Let sit for 15 minutes.

Pour squash and marinade onto a baking sheet.

Bake 25 to 30 minutes, or until squash is tender. (After 10 minutes, turn the squash pieces so they bake evenly.)

Per serving: 133 calories, 5 g fat, 23 g carbohydrates, 1 g fiber, 2 g protein

MUFFINS & BREADS

....

*To start baking gluten-free, use a gluten-*free oat flour or a gluten-free all-purpose flour. Gluten is the protein in wheat flour that holds baked goods together, so when you use GF all-purpose flour, you have to add xanthan gum or guar gum as a binding agent. *(Oat flour doesn't need a binder.)* If you are using a flour blend that includes a gum, omit the gum in the ingredient list. If your baked goods don't need to be gluten-free, you can substitute all-purpose flour for the flour listed; just remember to omit the xanthan gum if it's called for.

Oat Flour

Making your own oat flour is a cinch. Although gluten-free oat flour is becoming more available, both in stores and online, it's so easy to transform gluten-free oats into gluten-free oat flour that there's never an excuse not to bake up a lovely batch of muffins or cookies! If you grind up more than you need, you can keep the extra in a sealed container in your refrigerator for at least a month.

Makes 1 cup

1   cup gluten-free
    rolled oats

Grind oats in a blender, ¼ or ½ cup at a time, until they're the consistency of flour.

TIP Grinding small batches of oats (¼ cup at a time) will yield a finer flour, which I prefer. Using small batches, however, can be very time-consuming if you're making a large amount, so you can grind up to ½ cup at a time. The flour will have a coarser texture, but will still work well in the following recipes. If you put a whole cup of oats in your blender at one time, it will clog your blender and make it difficult to evenly grind the oats into flour.

Per cup: 307 calories, 5 g fat, 56 g carbohydrates, 8 g fiber, 11 g protein

Blueberry Muffins

These muffins will fill your kitchen with the most delicious aroma as they're baking. It's best to eat them warm from the oven, but they also taste great reheated for a few minutes in a 350°F oven.

Makes 12 muffins

2 cups gluten-free oat flour	¼ cup canola oil
1½ tsp baking powder, divided	¾ cup packed light brown sugar
½ tsp salt	½ tsp vanilla
½ cup applesauce	¼ cup rice milk
½ cup flaxseed meal	1½ cups blueberries (fresh or frozen)

Preheat oven to 350°F. Lightly oil a standard muffin pan.

In a medium bowl, combine oat flour, 1 teaspoon baking powder, and salt with a whisk.

In a large bowl, combine applesauce with ½ teaspoon baking powder. Add flaxseed meal, oil, brown sugar, vanilla, and rice milk to applesauce.

Slowly mix dry ingredients into applesauce mixture. Be careful not to overmix. Gently stir in blueberries. Spoon batter into prepared muffin pan. Bake 25–30 minutes or until a toothpick inserted into the center of a muffin comes out clean.

OAT-FREE VARIATION

Replace oat flour with 2 cups gluten-free all-purpose flour and 1 teaspoon xanthan gum. Increase vanilla from ½ teaspoon to 1 teaspoon.

Per muffin: 191 calories, 8 g fat, 29 g carbohydrates, 3 g fiber, 3 g protein

Autumn Pumpkin Muffins

Nothing says autumn as deliciously as warm-from-the-oven pumpkin muffins. These are particularly good with a cup of hot cider or tea. Topping them with Vanilla Frosting (page 188) or Coconut Frosting (page 190) makes a Halloween cupcake like no other!

Makes 12 muffins

2½ cups oat flour

2¼ tsps baking powder, divided

¾ tsp salt

1½ tsps cinnamon

½ tsp nutmeg

¾ cup applesauce

¼ cup canola oil

1 cup packed dark brown sugar

1 tsp vanilla

1 15-ounce can solid-packed pumpkin

½ cup dried sweetened cranberries (optional)

Preheat oven to 350°F. Oil a standard muffin pan.

In a small bowl, combine flour, 1½ teaspoons baking powder, salt, cinnamon, and nutmeg. Set aside.

In a large bowl, combine applesauce and ¾ teaspoon baking powder. Add oil, brown sugar, vanilla, and pumpkin. Add dry ingredients to pumpkin mixture, one half at a time. Stir to combine. Stir in cranberries.

Spoon into muffin pan. Bake 18–23 minutes, or until toothpick inserted in center of muffin comes out clean. Remove from pan; cool on rack.

OAT-FREE VARIATION

Replace oat flour with 2½ cups gluten-free all-purpose flour. Add one teaspoon xanthan gum to the dry ingredients.

Per muffin: 221 calories, 6 g fat, 40 g carbohydrates, 3 g fiber, 3 g protein

Coconut Chocolate Chip Mini Muffins

It's hard to know whether to call these muffins or cupcakes—they're so sweet and rich and full of flavor.

Makes 36 mini muffins

¾ cup shredded coconut

2   cups oat flour

1½ tsp baking powder, divided

½   tsp salt

½   cup applesauce

¼   cup coconut oil

½   cup flaxseed meal

¾   cup packed light brown sugar

½   cup coconut milk

1   cup allergy-free chocolate chips

Preheat oven to 350°F.

Spread coconut on a cookie sheet. Lightly toast in oven. Check every minute; it should take 2–3 minutes for coconut to turn a light gold. Remove from oven and set aside.

In a medium bowl, combine oat flour, 1 teaspoon baking powder, and salt, using a whisk.

In a large bowl, combine applesauce and ½ teaspoon baking powder. Melt coconut oil in microwave or on the stove. Add melted oil to applesauce. Add flaxseed meal, brown sugar, and coconut milk to applesauce.

Slowly mix dry ingredients into applesauce mixture. Mix in chocolate chips and toasted coconut. Spoon into oiled mini muffin pan. Bake 15 minutes, or until a toothpick inserted into a muffin comes out clean.

OAT-FREE VARIATION

Replace oat flour with 2 cups gluten-free all-purpose flour plus 1 teaspoon xanthan gum.

Per muffin: 99 calories, 5 g fat, 13 g carbohydrates, 1 g fiber, 1 g protein

Apple-Zucchini Mini Muffins

You can make any muffin in either a mini or standard size muffin tin. As a rule of thumb, standard-size muffins take about twice as long to bake as mini muffins.

24 mini muffins

2	cups oat flour	2	tbsps coconut oil
1½	tsps baking powder, divided	1	tsp vanilla
1¼	tsps cinnamon	¼	cup agave nectar
1	tsp baking soda	1	cup peeled and chopped apples
½	tsp salt	1	cup shredded zucchini
½	cup applesauce		

Preheat oven to 375°F. Oil a mini muffin pan.

In a medium bowl, combine oat flour, 1 teaspoon baking powder, cinnamon, baking soda, and salt.

In a large bowl, combine applesauce with ½ teaspoon baking powder. Add coconut oil, vanilla, and agave nectar to applesauce. Stir to combine thoroughly.

Mix dry ingredients into applesauce. Add apples and zucchini to batter. Stir to combine. Spoon into prepared mini muffin pan. Bake 12–15 minutes, or until a toothpick inserted in the center of a muffin comes out clean.

OAT-FREE VARIATION

Replace oat flour with 2 cups gluten-free all-purpose flour and 1 teaspoon xanthan gum.

Per muffin: 56 calories, 2 g fat, 9 g carbohydrates, 1 g fiber, 1 g protein

Butternut Squash-Blueberry Mini Muffins

These little treats are nutrition powerhouses. They get their sweetness from agave nectar and blueberries, making them a great choice for snackers who need a low-sugar treat. My friend Liz makes these muffins using butternut squash baby food. Delicious!

Makes 24 mini muffins

1¼ cups cornmeal

1 cup gluten-free all-purpose flour

2 tsps baking powder, divided

½ tsp xanthan gum

1 tsp cinnamon

1 tsp baking soda

½ tsp salt

½ cup applesauce

1 cup butternut squash (cubed, steamed, and mashed)

2 tbsps canola oil

1 tsp vanilla

¼ cup agave nectar

1 cup blueberries (fresh or frozen)

Preheat oven to 400°F. Oil a mini muffin pan.

In a medium bowl, combine cornmeal, flour, 1½ teaspoons baking powder, xanthan gum, cinnamon, baking soda, and salt.

In a large bowl, combine applesauce with ½ teaspoon baking powder. Add squash, oil, vanilla, and agave nectar to applesauce.

Mix dry ingredients into squash mixture. Mixture will be pretty dry.

Mix blueberries into batter.

Spoon into muffin pan. Bake 12–15 minutes, or until golden, and a toothpick inserted into the center of a muffin comes out clean.

Muffins & Breads

Per muffin: 79 calories, 2 g fat, 16 g carbohydrates, 1 g fiber, 1 g protein

Country Corn Muffins

These muffins are the perfect complement to a bowl of soup, chili, or salad. They also make a great breakfast or snack, warmed up and served with a little jam or honey. Using coarse cornmeal (polenta) will provide a nice crunchiness, while finer cornmeal will yield a more delicate texture.

Makes 12 muffins

1	cup cornmeal
1	cup gluten-free all-purpose flour
½	cup granulated sugar
2¼	tsps baking powder, divided
1	tsp baking soda
½	tsp salt
1	tsp xanthan gum
¼	cup applesauce
1⅓	cup rice milk
3	tbsps canola oil
1	cup corn kernels (fresh or frozen)

Preheat oven to 400°F. Lightly oil standard muffin pan.

In a medium bowl, combine cornmeal, flour, sugar, 2 teaspoons baking powder, baking soda, salt, and xanthan gum.

In a separate bowl, combine applesauce with ¼ teaspoon baking powder. Add rice milk and canola oil to applesauce.

Slowly mix dry ingredients into applesauce.

Add corn; stir until blended.

Spoon batter into muffin pan. Bake 18–22 minutes, until a toothpick inserted into muffin comes out clean.

Per muffin: 173 calories, 4 g fat, 32 g carbohydrates, 2 g fiber, 2 g protein

Peach Raspberry Muffins

These muffins have a light, summery flavor. They store well in the refrigerator for three or four days, but taste best if reheated for a few minutes in a 350°F oven.

Makes 12 muffins

2   cups gluten-free all-purpose flour

1   tsp xanthan gum

1½   tsps baking powder, divided

½   tsp salt

½   cup pureed peaches

⅓   cup canola oil

½   cup flaxseed meal

¾   cup packed light brown sugar

¼   cup rice milk

¼   cup orange juice

1½   cups raspberries (fresh or frozen)

Preheat oven to 350°F. Oil a standard muffin pan.

In a medium bowl, combine flour, xanthan gum, 1 teaspoon baking powder, and salt.

In a large bowl, combine peaches with ½ teaspoon baking powder. Add oil, flaxseed meal, brown sugar, rice milk, and orange juice.

Slowly mix dry ingredients into peach mixture.

Gently mix in raspberries.

Spoon batter into pan. Bake 25–30 minutes or until a tester inserted into the center of a muffin comes out clean.

Per muffin: 179 calories, 9 g fat, 25 g carbohydrates, 5 g fiber, 3 g protein

Sandwich Muffins

These muffins take the place of a sandwich in your lunch bag.
Add a coconut-based yogurt and sliced red peppers and you've got
a complete lunch.

Makes 12 muffins

2 cups gluten-free oat flour	½ cup flaxseed meal
1½ tsp baking powder, divided	¾ cup brown sugar
½ tsp salt	1 tsp vanilla
1½ cups fresh or frozen strawberries	½ cup rice milk
½ cup applesauce	¾ cup Sunflower Seed Butter (page 14)

Preheat oven to 350°F. Oil a standard muffin pan.

In a medium bowl, combine oat flour, 1 teaspoon baking powder, and salt.

Finely chop strawberries.

In a large bowl, combine applesauce with ½ teaspoon baking powder.
Add flaxseed meal, brown sugar, vanilla, rice milk, and sunflower seed
butter to applesauce.

Mix dry ingredients into applesauce mixture. Gently stir in strawberries.
Spoon into muffin tin. Bake 25–30 minutes, or until toothpick inserted
into muffin comes out dry.

OAT-FREE VARIATION

Replace oat flour with 2 cups gluten-free all-purpose flour plus
1 teaspoon xanthan gum.

Per muffin: 242 calories, 11 g fat, 33 g carbohydrates, 3 g fiber, 6 g protein

Double Chocolate Zucchini Muffins

The only thing that's muffin-y about these rich muffins is the texture. My boys call them cupcakes. They are truly dessert-worthy.

Makes 15 muffins

3	cups gluten-free oat flour	¾	cup packed brown sugar
1	tsp baking soda	¾	cup granulated sugar
1¾	tsps baking powder, divided	¼	cup canola oil
1	tsp salt	1	tbsp vanilla
¼	cup plus 2 tbsps cocoa powder	2	cups raw grated zucchini
¾	cup applesauce	1	cup chocolate chips

Preheat oven to 350°F. Oil two muffin pans (or one, and use twice).

In a medium bowl, combine oat flour, baking soda, 1 teaspoon baking powder, salt, and cocoa powder; stir with a whisk.

In a large bowl, combine applesauce with ¾ teaspoon baking powder. Add sugars, oil, and vanilla to applesauce. Thoroughly mix zucchini into applesauce mixture.

Mix dry ingredients into zucchini mixture. Stir chocolate chips into batter.

Spoon into oiled muffin pan. Bake 20–25 minutes, or until a toothpick inserted in the center of a muffin comes out clean.

OAT-FREE VARIATION

Replace the oat flour with 3 cups gluten-free all-purpose flour and 1½ teaspoons xanthan gum.

Per serving: 259 calories, 10 g fat, 43 g carbohydrates, 2 g fiber, 4 g protein

Carrot Cake Muffins

If you want to turn these muffins into cupcakes, top them with Vanilla or Coconut Frosting (pages 188 and 190) instead of cinnamon-sugar topping.

Makes 12 muffins

2	cups gluten-free oat flour	¼	cup canola oil
1½	tsp baking powder, divided	¾	cup packed light brown sugar
½	tsp salt	½	tsp vanilla
2	tsps cinnamon, divided	¼	cup rice milk
½	cup applesauce	2	cups grated carrots
½	cup flaxseed meal	2	tsps granulated sugar

Preheat oven to 350°F. Lightly oil a standard muffin pan.

In a medium bowl, using a whisk, combine oat flour, 1 teaspoon baking powder, salt, and 1 teaspoon cinnamon.

In a large bowl, combine applesauce and ½ teaspoon baking powder. Add flaxseed meal, canola oil, brown sugar, vanilla, and rice milk.

Slowly mix dry ingredients into applesauce. Be careful not to overmix. Stir in grated carrots.

Spoon batter into prepared muffin pan. In a small bowl, combine 1 teaspoon cinnamon and granulated sugar. Sprinkle on top of muffin batter. Bake 25–30 minutes or until a toothpick inserted into the center of a muffin comes out clean.

OAT-FREE VARIATION

Replace oat flour with 2 cups gluten-free all-purpose flour plus 1 teaspoon xanthan gum. Increase vanilla from ½ teaspoon to 1 teaspoon.

Per muffin: 154 calories, 8 g fat, 19 g carbohydrates, 3 g fiber, 3 g protein

Apple Pie Muffins

If you want a deeper, richer sugar flavor, use dark brown sugar; light brown sugar will be less intense.

Makes 12 muffins

2 cups gluten-free oat flour	½ cup flaxseed meal
1½ tsps baking powder, divided	¼ cup canola oil
½ tsp salt	¾ cup packed brown sugar
½ tsp cinnamon	¼ cup rice milk
¼ tsp nutmeg	1½ cups chopped apples
½ cup applesauce	

Preheat oven to 350°F. Oil a standard muffin pan.

In a medium bowl, combine oat flour, 1 teaspoon baking powder, salt, cinnamon, and nutmeg. Stir with a whisk.

In a large bowl, combine applesauce with ½ teaspoon baking powder. Add flaxseed meal, oil, brown sugar, and rice milk.

Mix dry ingredients into applesauce, one half at a time. Add apples. Stir to combine.

Divide batter into muffin pan. Bake 25–30 minutes, or until a toothpick inserted into the middle of a muffin comes out clean.

OAT-FREE VARIATION

Replace oat flour with 2 cups gluten-free all-purpose flour plus 1 teaspoon xanthan gum.

Per muffin: 186 calories, 7 g fat, 28 g carbohydrates, 3 g fiber, 3 g protein

Raspberry Cranberry Muffins

Dried cherries work as well as cranberries in this recipe. You can also replace the raspberries with strawberries, depending on your preference.

Makes 12 muffins

2 cups gluten-free oat flour	¾ cup packed brown sugar
1½ tsps baking powder, divided	½ tsp vanilla
½ tsp salt	¼ cup rice milk
½ cup applesauce	1 cup raspberries (fresh or frozen)
½ cup flaxseed meal	½ cup dried, sweetened cranberries
¼ cup canola oil	

Preheat oven to 350°F.

In a medium bowl, combine oat flour, 1 teaspoon baking powder, and salt. Stir using a whisk.

In a large bowl, combine applesauce with ½ teaspoon baking powder. Add flaxseed meal, canola oil, brown sugar, vanilla, and rice milk to applesauce.

Slowly mix dry ingredients into applesauce mixture. Be careful not to overmix. Stir raspberries and cranberries into batter. Spoon batter into prepared muffin pan. Bake 25–30 minutes or until a toothpick inserted into the center of a muffin comes out clean.

OAT-FREE VARIATION

Replace oat flour with 2 cups gluten-free all-purpose flour and 1 teaspoon xanthan gum. Increase vanilla to 1 teaspoon.

Per muffin: 220 calories, 9 g fat, 33 g carbohydrates, 5 g fiber, 4 g protein

Pineapple-Strawberry Mini Muffins

You can substitute fresh fruit for frozen when it's available.

Makes 24 mini muffins

2 cups gluten-free oat flour	1 tsp vanilla
1½ tsps baking powder, divided	3 tbsps agave nectar
½ tsp salt	½ cup light coconut milk
½ cup applesauce	1 cup frozen pineapple chunks
½ cup flaxseed meal	1 cup frozen strawberries
¼ cup coconut oil	

Preheat oven 350°F. Oil a mini muffin pan.

In a medium bowl, combine oat flour, 1 teaspoon baking powder, and salt, using a whisk.

In a large bowl, combine applesauce with ½ teaspoon baking powder. Add flaxseed meal, coconut oil, vanilla, agave nectar, and coconut milk to applesauce.

Slowly mix dry ingredients into applesauce mixture. Be careful not to overmix.

In a food processor, finely chop pineapple and strawberries. Add to batter. Scoop into mini muffin pan. Bake 15–18 minutes.

OAT-FREE VARIATION

Replace oat flour with two cups gluten-free all-purpose flour and 1 teaspoon xanthan gum.

Per muffin: 87 calories, 4 g fat, 11 g carbohydrates, 2 g fiber, 2 g protein

Beer Bread

Gluten-free baking can be a challenge, particularly when you are working with yeast. This beer bread bakes up crusty and flavorful without the complication of proofing, rising, and kneading bread dough. Keep in mind that although some of the alcohol from the beer burns off in the baking, some does remain. Several gluten-free beers are available. If your local liquor store doesn't stock any, ask the manager to order a few and become a hero to your gluten-free neighbors!

Makes 1 loaf, about 12 slices

1½ tbsps olive oil, divided

3 cups gluten-free all-purpose flour

½ tsp xanthan gum

1½ tsps salt

½ cup granulated sugar

1½ tsps baking powder

1 12-ounce gluten-free beer

Preheat oven to 375°F. Liberally oil a loaf pan with olive oil. Reserve remaining oil.

In a large bowl, use a whisk to combine flour, xanthan gum, salt, sugar, and baking powder. Mix in beer.

Scrape batter into oiled pan. Brush top of bread with remaining oil.

Bake 50 minutes or until crust is golden and crusty.

Per slice: 161 calories, 3 g fat, 32 g carbohydrates, 3 g fiber, 3 g protein

Oat-Cornmeal Bread

Spread sunflower-seed butter or hummus on this bread for a great flavor. After the first day, oat-cornmeal bread tastes best toasted.

Makes one loaf (12 slices)

2	cups oat flour
1	cup cornmeal
½	cup sugar
1½	tsps baking powder
1½	tsps salt
¼	tsp xanthan gum
12	ounces gluten-free beer
2	tbsps old-fashioned gluten-free rolled oats
	canola oil for pan

Preheat oven to 375°F. Spray or brush canola oil in a bread pan.

In a large bowl, combine flour, cornmeal, sugar, baking powder, salt, and xanthan gum. Mix beer into flour mixture.

Pour batter into oiled pan. Sprinkle oats on top.

Bake 55–60 minutes, or until loaf is golden. Cool on a cooling rack.

Muffins & Breads

Per slice: 154 calories, 2 g fat, 30 g carbohydrates, 2 g fiber, 3 g protein

Zucchini Bread

At our house, we call this breakfast cake (or lunch cake or dinner cake or snack cake). For a more dessert-y version, add ½ to ¾ cup chocolate chips to the batter. Zucchini Bread freezes nicely and makes great toast after it thaws. It's delicious at room temperature, too.

Makes 2 loaves (16 slices each)

3	cups oat flour	¼	cup canola oil
1	tsp baking soda	1½	cups granulated sugar
1¾	tsp baking powder, divided	½	cup flaxseed meal
1	tsp salt	1	tbsp vanilla
1	tsp cinnamon	2	cups raw grated zucchini
¾	cup applesauce		

Preheat oven to 350°F. Oil two loaf pans.

In a medium bowl, combine oat flour, baking soda, 1 teaspoon baking powder, salt, and cinnamon, using a whisk.

In a large bowl, combine applesauce with ¾ teaspoon baking powder. Add oil, sugar, flaxseed meal, vanilla, and zucchini to applesauce. Add dry ingredients to zucchini mixture. Combine thoroughly.

Pour into greased loaf pans. Bake for 60–70 minutes. Breads are done when a tester inserted in the middle comes out dry. Cool for 10 minutes before removing from pans. Cool completely.

OAT-FREE VARIATION

Substitute 3 cups gluten-free all-purpose flour and 1½ teaspoons xanthan gum for the oat flour.

Per slice: 131 calories, 5 g fat, 23 g carbohydrates, 1 g fiber, 1 g protein

Corn Tortillas

Masa harina is a corn flour that is specially processed for making tortillas. You can find it in the Mexican-food aisle at the grocery store.

Makes 16 tortillas

2   cups masa harina

1¼ cups water

Blend ingredients until the mixture sticks together, but isn't really wet.

Roll into 16 small balls; cover with a damp cloth. Press dough, one ball at a time, between wax paper in a tortilla press. If you don't have a tortilla press, either flatten each ball into a disc in your hands, or roll out each ball with a rolling pin until the disc is ⅛ inch thick.

Heat each tortilla individually in a dry skillet, flipping it over when cooked on one side.

Keep tortillas warm in a 200°F oven until all the tortillas are done.

Muffins & Breads

Per tortilla: 73 calories, 0 g fat, 16 g carbohydrates, 1 g fiber, 1 g protein

Biscuits

Biscuits are truly a multi-purpose bread. My husband likes them dipped in soup, while the boys like them spread with jam. You can also slice biscuits in half and use them to make mini sandwiches.

Makes 8 biscuits

1½ cups gluten-free
    all-purpose flour

1   tsp baking powder

½   tsp baking soda

¼   tsp salt

½   tsp xanthan gum

¼   cup all-vegetable
    shortening

1   cup rice milk

1   tsp lemon juice

Preheat oven to 425°F.

In a large bowl, combine flour, baking powder, baking soda, salt, and xanthan gum using a whisk.

Cut shortening into flour mixture using a pastry cutter or two knives.

In a small bowl, combine rice milk and lemon juice. Add liquid to flour mixture; stir to combine.

Drop heaping tablespoons of batter onto ungreased cookie sheets.

Bake 12–15 minutes, or until golden.

Per biscuit: 148 calories, 7 g fat, 20 g carbohydrates, 2 g fiber, 2 g protein

Sweet Potato Biscuits

Sweet potatoes add lots of vitamins and creaminess to these biscuits, so you can use less fat than in traditional biscuits. You can use canned sweet potato puree or even sweet potato baby food if you don't have any sweet potatoes in your pantry.

Makes 16 biscuits

3	cups oat flour
2½	tsps baking powder, divided
1	tsp baking soda
½	tsp salt
½	cup applesauce
1	cup cooked, mashed sweet potato
2	tbsps olive oil
⅜	cup rice milk

Preheat oven to 425°F.

In a medium bowl, combine flour, 2 teaspoons baking powder, baking soda, and salt.

In a large bowl, combine applesauce with ½ teaspoon baking powder. Add sweet potato, olive oil, and rice milk to applesauce. Stir well.

Mix dry ingredients into sweet potato mixture.

Drop heaping tablespoons of batter onto greased cookie sheets.

Bake 15–18 minutes.

Per biscuit: 103 calories, 3 g fat, 16 g carbohydrates, 1 g fiber, 3 g protein

BREAKFASTS

. . . .

Why not start your day with a delicious breakfast? There are so many options, whether you're feeding just yourself or a crowd, that breakfast can be the best part of the day! I love whipping up pancakes on a weekend morning. It transports me to the best times of my childhood. Why rush through the start of your day when you can get all messy and way-too-full? And who can be crabby with a belly full of goodness?

Granola

Why settle for one or two kinds of cereal the supermarket can provide when you can have this delicious, filling granola in less than half an hour? Not only is it good with rice milk for breakfast, granola also makes a crunchy topping for sorbet, coconut-based yogurt, and applesauce.

Makes 4 cups

2   cups oats

⅓   cup shelled pumpkin seeds (pepitas), finely chopped

¼   cup shelled sunflower seeds, finely chopped

¼   cup apple juice

¼   cup maple syrup

2   tbsps canola oil

1   tsp cinnamon

½   cup raisins (or your favorite dried fruit)

Preheat oven to 350°F.

Combine oats, seeds, apple juice, maple syrup, oil, and cinnamon.

Spread on a greased cookie sheet. Bake 15–20 minutes, or until golden brown.

When cool, combine with raisins.

Per ½ cup serving: 223 calories, 10 g fat, 32 g carbohydrate, 3 g fiber, 5 g protein

Sunday Morning Pancakes

The combination of oats and cornmeal in these pancakes makes a delicious, slightly crunchy breakfast treat. For an extra blast of flavor, serve these pancakes with Blueberry Syrup (page 167), Peach Compote (page 168), or pure maple syrup.

Makes 16 3½-inch pancakes

2	cups gluten-free oat flour
½	cup cornmeal (polenta will add a bit of crunch; fine cornmeal will provide less)
¼	cup sugar
2½	tsps baking powder, divided
2	tsps baking soda
¼	tsp salt
½	cup applesauce
2¼	cups rice milk
2	tbsps canola oil
1	tsp vanilla
	oil for brushing

Preheat oven to 200°F.

In a small bowl, combine oat flour, cornmeal, sugar, 2 teaspoons baking powder, baking soda, and salt using a whisk.

In a large bowl, combine applesauce and ½ teaspoon baking powder. Add rice milk, canola oil, and vanilla to applesauce. Add dry ingredients.

Lightly brush a frying pan with oil. Heat pan until a drop of water dances on the surface. Pour a generous portion (about ¼ cup) of batter into pan. Cook until bubbles form on surface. Flip pancake and cook on other side.

Keep pancakes warm in oven while cooking remaining pancakes.

TIP For a nice variation, especially in the late spring and early summer, add 1 cup of fresh blueberries to the batter. If you use frozen blueberries, your pancake batter will turn a bluish-purple color.

Per cup serving: 112 calories, 3 g fat, 19 g carbohydrate, 1 g fiber, 2 g protein

Breakfasts

Biscuit-Based French Toast

Special occasions—or just Sunday mornings—call for special breakfasts. Serve this hearty biscuit-based French toast with maple syrup, Blueberry Syrup (page 167), or Peach Compote (page 168) for an extra-special treat.

Makes 16 pieces

8	Biscuits (page 160)
1	6-ounce container vanilla coconut-based yogurt (or rice-based yogurt)
½	cup rice milk
½	tsp vanilla
¼	tsp cinnamon
2	tsps coconut oil, divided (or soy-free, nonhydrogenated vegan margarine)

Preheat oven to 200°F.

Slice biscuits in half length-wise.

In a shallow bowl, combine yogurt, rice milk, vanilla, and cinnamon.

Heat 1 teaspoon of the coconut oil in a medium-size skillet or griddle pan.

Working with one piece at a time, coat biscuit on both sides with batter. Cook biscuits in hot oil. Flip biscuits over when they're golden on one side, after about 2 minutes.

Keep biscuits warm in oven until all pieces are cooked.

Per 2-piece serving: 182 calories, 10 g fat, 23 g carbohydrates, 3 g fiber, 3 g protein

Blueberry Syrup

You can use this technique to make syrup from any fruits—not just blueberries. If you have any left over, store it in a lidded jar in the refrigerator for up to a week. Fruit syrups are delicious on— or in—just about everything, from pancakes and crepes to sorbets and shakes.

Makes about ¾ cup

1   cup blueberries

1   cup plus 2 tsps water, divided

1   tbsp agave nectar

½   tsp vanilla

1   tsp cornstarch

In a small saucepan, combine blueberries with 1 cup water, agave nectar, and vanilla. Bring to a boil over medium-high heat until reduced by slightly more than half.

In a small bowl, combine cornstarch with 2 teaspoons cold water. Add cornstarch mixture to blueberries.

Stir until the mixture has a syrup consistency.

Per 2 tbsp serving: 27 calories, 0 g fat, 7 g carbohydrates, 1 g fiber, 0 g protein

Peach Compote

This compote has such an opulent flavor it can turn a plain bowl of sorbet into a company dessert.

Makes about ½ cup

1	cup fresh peach slices
1	cup water
1	tbsp agave nectar
⅛	tsp cinnamon

In a small saucepan, combine all ingredients. Simmer over medium-high heat 15–20 minutes or until peaches are soft.

Break peaches up into small pieces with a spoon and serve over your favorite sorbet.

Per serving: 121 calories, 0 g fat, 31 g carbohydrates, 3 g fiber, 1 g protein

Not Quite Instant Oatmeal

Basic oatmeal is your starting point for making delicious, nutritious hot breakfasts that take only minutes to prepare. To get your day off to a great start, try one of the variations below.

Makes 2 servings

1 cup gluten-free old-fashioned rolled oats	In a small saucepan, combine oats and water. Bring to a boil; reduce heat to a simmer.
1¾ cups water	Cook 3–5 minutes until creamy.

Per serving: 170 calories, 3 g fat, 31 g carbohydrates, 4 g fiber, 6 g protein

---

BANANA OATMEAL

If you love warm banana bread, this oatmeal will deliver much of the same delicious flavor—with a lot less effort!

Makes 2 servings

1 cup prepared oatmeal	Sprinkle brown sugar on warm oatmeal. Mix in bananas. Top with warm rice milk.
2 tsps brown sugar	
¼ cup thinly sliced, then quartered banana	
¼ cup rice milk	

Per serving: 123 calories, 2 g fat, 25 g carbohydrates, 2 g fiber, 3 g protein

Breakfasts

CRANBERRY-PUMPKIN SEED OATMEAL

This oatmeal combines sweet and savory flavors with smooth and crunchy textures.

Makes 2 servings

1	cup prepared oatmeal
¼	cup dried sweetened cranberries
1	tbsp shelled pumpkin seeds (pepitas)
2	tsps brown sugar
¼	cup rice milk, warmed

Toast pumpkin seeds in a dry frying pan over medium heat until fragrant, but not browned (approximately 30 seconds).

Mix cranberries, pumpkin seeds, and brown sugar into warm oatmeal.

Top with warm rice milk.

Per serving: 173 calories, 24 g fat, 33 g carbohydrates, 3 g fiber, 4 g protein

CREAMY STRAWBERRY OATMEAL

Strawberry preserves provide sweetness and additional texture to this variation.

Makes 2 servings

1	cup prepared oatmeal
¼	cup strawberries, diced
2	tbsps all-fruit strawberry preserves
¼	cup light coconut milk

Mix strawberries and preserves into warm oatmeal.

Top oatmeal with warm coconut milk.

Per serving: 172 calories, 5 g fat, 31 g carbohydrates, 3 g fiber, 3 g protein

APPLE CINNAMON OATMEAL

My sons, Casey and Evan, love this flavor combination.

Makes 2 servings

1	cup prepared oatmeal
¼	cup diced apples
¼	tsp cinnamon
2	tsps brown sugar
¼	cup rice milk

Mix apples, cinnamon, and brown sugar into warm oatmeal.

Top oatmeal with warm rice milk.

Per serving: 115 calories, 2 g fat, 23 g carbohydrates, 2 g fiber, 3 g protein

Chocolate Banana Smoothie

This smoothie is chocolate-y enough for dessert. It makes a great snack, too.

Makes 2 servings

4   tsps cocoa

1   tsp granulated sugar

1½ frozen bananas

⅓   cup sunflower seed butter

⅓   cup apple juice

2   cups rice milk

In a small bowl, mix together cocoa and sugar. Slowly add boiling water, one tablespoon at a time, to make a thin paste.

Combine banana, sunflower seed butter, apple juice, rice milk, and chocolate paste in blender. Blend until smooth.

Add more rice milk for a thinner smoothie.

Per serving: 479 calories, 24 g fat, 64 g carbohydrates, 4 g fiber, 11 g protein

Good Morning Smoothie

This basic fruit smoothie recipe can be adapted to almost any fruit combination. Experiment with the ones you like best. Whenever you have a banana that's about to turn—don't toss it. Instead, peel and store it in a plastic baggie in the freezer. The next time you want a banana for a smoothie, you'll have it. Don't worry if it gets discolored; your smoothie will look lovely (and taste even better) with the addition of other colorful fruits.

Makes 4 servings

1 cup frozen pineapple chunks	Combine pineapple chunks, banana, strawberries, and rice milk in blender. Blend until smooth.
1 frozen banana	
1 cup frozen strawberries	Adjust consistency with apple juice.
2 cups rice milk	
½ cup apple juice	

Per serving: 140 calories, 1 g fat, 32 g carbohydrates, 3 g fiber, 1 g protein

Strawberry Cantaloupe Smoothie

Use summer cantaloupe when it's at its sweetest. Cut it in chunks and store it in the freezer for the next time you want a cool and delicious treat.

Makes 4 servings

1½ cups frozen strawberries	Combine in blender. Blend until smooth.
1½ cups frozen cantaloupe chunks	Add a little extra apple juice for a thinner consistency.
2 cups rice milk	
½ cup apple juice	

Per serving: 126 calories, 2 g fat, 28 g carbohydrates, 2 g fiber, 1 g protein

Crepes

These thin, tasty pancakes are great for breakfast (pile them high and pour on the maple syrup!) or as dessert with a sweet fruit filling. You can also serve them as a savory dinner entrée with delicious fillings such as Mixed Mushroom Sauté (page 19) or Creamed Spinach (page 138).

Makes 4 or 5 crepes

½	cup rice milk	1	cup oat flour
½	cup water	2	tbsps sugar
¼	cup coconut oil, melted	¼	tsp salt

In a medium bowl, combine rice milk, water, and melted coconut oil.

Mix in oat flour, sugar, and salt. Stir until smooth.

Heat a small (4–5 inch) nonstick pan over medium heat. Pour about 3 tablespoons batter into pan. Swirl to spread evenly in pan.

Cook until edges firm up; then flip crepe. Cook on other side.
Crepes cook quickly; they should be lightly golden and cooked through.
Let them cool on a piece of wax paper until ready to serve.
Fill with the filling of your choice.

TIP If you're serving these crepes with a savory filling, decrease the sugar to your taste.

OAT-FREE VARIATION

Substitute 1 cup gluten-free flour plus 1 teaspoon xanthan gum for the oat flour.

Per crepe: 192 calories, 13 g fat, 18 g carbohydrates, 1 g fiber, 3 g protein

Mixed Berry Crepes

Top these delicious crepes with powdered sugar or Coconut Crème (page 198).

Makes 4 crepes

1   *cup all-fruit blueberry preserves*

1   *cup berries (blueberries, blackberries, and/or sliced strawberries)*

2   *tbsps cornstarch*

2   *tbsps cold water*

4   *Crepes (page 175)*

Combine preserves and fruit in a small saucepan. Bring to a boil.

In a separate bowl, combine cornstarch and water, stirring until cornstarch is completely dissolved.

Once fruit mixture is boiling, add cornstarch and reduce heat to simmer. Stir until thickened.

Place one crepe in the center of a small plate. Spoon filling onto one side. Wrap crepe over the filling.

Per serving: 484 calories, 16 g fat, 83 g carbohydrates, 3 g fiber, 4 g protein

Doughnut Bites

When I realized that my six-year-old (who has food allergies) had never eaten a doughnut, I knew I had to do something about it... and quick! These tasty bites have a great doughnut flavor and texture and are especially delicious topped with chocolate glaze. If you really want a complete doughnut experience, you can buy a mini doughnut pan on the Internet or at a specialty baking shop. If you just want a doughnut-y snack, you can bake these in a mini muffin pan. Be careful not to fill the cups to the rim, though, or the batter will blow up into a muffin shape.

Makes 30 doughnut bites

1	cup gluten-free all-purpose flour	⅛	tsp cinnamon
¼	tsp xanthan gum	¼	cup applesauce
½	cup granulated sugar	½	cup rice milk
1¾	tsps baking powder, divided	½	tsp vanilla
¼	tsp salt	½	tsp apple cider vinegar
¼	tsp nutmeg	¼	cup canola oil

Preheat oven to 350°F. Lightly oil a mini muffin pan (or two depending on the size).

In a medium bowl, combine flour, xanthan gum, sugar, 1½ teaspoons baking powder, salt, nutmeg, and cinnamon.

In a large bowl, combine applesauce with ¼ teaspoon baking powder. Add rice milk, vanilla, vinegar, and oil to applesauce.

continued

Mix dry ingredients into applesauce mixture. Spoon into mini muffin pan, filling two-thirds full. If you overfill the cups, the doughnuts will puff up and look like mini muffins instead.

Bake 12 minutes, or until a toothpick inserted into the center comes out clean.

Turn doughnut bites out of pan onto a cutting board or baking board. Let cool completely before glazing.

CHOCOLATE GLAZE

½   cup powdered sugar

2   tbsps cocoa

½   tsp vanilla

1   tbsp plus 1 tsp rice milk

In a small bowl, combine sugar and cocoa. Add vanilla and rice milk. Stir until smooth.

Dip the top of each doughnut bite into the glaze. Let glaze dry before serving.

TIP You can top doughnut bites with colored sprinkles while the glaze is still wet. Just make sure they're safe for your guests.

Per serving: 46 calories, 2 g fat, 7 g carbohydrates, 0 g fiber, 0 g protein

Brunch Hash

While my boys love sweet breakfasts like pancakes and French toast, my husband and I really love to dig into a savory breakfast. This hash had our tasters begging for more!

Makes 6 servings

1	cup buckwheat (roasted kasha)
2	cups water
1	vegan gluten-free bouillon cube
2	green peppers, chopped
1	onion, chopped
4	potatoes, chopped
2	tbsps olive oil, divided
2	tbsps nutritional yeast
½	tsp salt
	freshly ground black pepper
1	tbsp fresh thyme

Preheat oven to 425°F.

In a small saucepan, combine buckwheat, water, and bouillon cube. Bring to a boil, cover, reduce heat, and cook for 10 minutes, or until all the liquid is absorbed.

While the buckwheat is cooking, combine peppers, onion, and potatoes in a large bowl. Add 1 tablespoon olive oil, nutritional yeast, salt, and pepper to vegetables. Spread on a baking sheet. Bake for 10 minutes.

Heat remaining tablespoon of olive oil in a large sauté pan over medium-high heat. Add thyme and cook for 1 minute. Add vegetables and kasha. Stir to combine.

Per serving: 291 calories, 5 g fat, 54 g carbohydrates, 5 g fiber, 9 g protein

Vegetable Chilaquiles

This is a meal that's hard to categorize, because it makes a wonderful dinner or lunch entrée, as well as a savory breakfast dish. The lime-scented topping works well on other Mexican- or Caribbean-influenced dishes, too.

Makes 6 servings

1   poblano pepper

1   green bell pepper

1   red bell pepper

1   tbsp olive oil

8–10 mushrooms, sliced

1   15-ounce can black beans, drained and rinsed

1   cup salsa

4   handfuls tortilla chips

1   container plain-flavored coconut-based yogurt

zest of one lime

chopped cilantro for garnish

Preheat broiler.

Remove stems, seeds, and membranes from peppers. Broil peppers skin side up until skin is blackened and bubbly. Place peppers into a sealed container or plastic bag. Set aside.

In a large skillet or sauté pan, heat olive oil over medium-high heat. Add mushrooms and black beans. Sauté 3–5 minutes.

While mushrooms and beans are cooking, remove skins from peppers and chop into large dice. Add peppers to mushrooms and beans. Add salsa and stir to thoroughly coat vegetables with salsa.

Roughly crumble tortilla chips and add to vegetables. Stir to toss.

In a small bowl, combine yogurt and lime zest. Garnish bowls of chilaquiles with cilantro and lime-scented yogurt.

Per serving: 225 calories, 8 g fat, 32 g carbohydrates, 8 g fiber, 8 g protein

Hash Browns

This classic breakfast staple pairs deliciously with fresh, warm muffins and Sausage Patties (page 89) for a special brunch.

Makes 6 servings

6   small potatoes

1   green pepper

1   onion

1   tsp salt

2   tbsps canola oil, divided

Shred the vegetables and combine them in a large bowl. (A food processor works well for this.) Toss the vegetables with salt and let them sit for at least 10 minutes. Drain excess liquid.

Heat half of the canola oil in a large skillet or griddle pan over medium heat. Working in batches, spread a thin layer of vegetables over the surface of the pan. Scrape and flip the vegetables as they cook and brown. Add more oil as necessary to keep the vegetables from sticking.

Per serving: 197 calories, 5 g fat, 36 g carbohydrates, 3 g fiber, 4 g protein

DESSERTS

....

The Lutz family LOVES dessert! Luckily, the *Welcoming Kitchen* offers lots of options when you're craving something sweet. You will be the hit of the potluck if you bring along one of these treats. Planning ahead can save a lot of time and heartache. I bake up a bunch of cupcakes, then individually wrap and freeze them, so that when I need a safe treat for a birthday party or other celebration, I just thaw a few cupcakes, top them with a sprinkle of powdered sugar or a little frosting, and save the day!

Chocolate Birthday Cake

Even my picky-eater dad loves this chocolate-y cake. When you need to bring a special treat to a friend's house, bake this cake in a square pan, sprinkle powdered sugar over the top of the cooled cake, and cut it into squares. (This recipe also makes 6 large or 9 small cupcakes.)

Makes one 8- or 9-inch cake

1½   cups gluten-free all-purpose flour
½   tsp xanthan gum
⅓   cup unsweetened cocoa powder
1   tsp baking soda
½   tsp salt
1   cup granulated sugar

½   cup canola oil
1   cup brewed coffee (decaf is fine)
2   tsps vanilla extract
2   tbsps apple cider vinegar
½   cup allergy-free chocolate chips

Preheat oven to 375°F.

Using a whisk, stir together flour, xanthan gum, cocoa, baking soda, salt, and sugar. Mix in oil, coffee, and vanilla. Stir until combined. Stir in vinegar.

Pour one third of the batter into a greased cake pan.

Stir chocolate chips into remaining batter. Add the rest of the batter to the pan.

Bake 25–30 minutes, or until a tester inserted into the center comes out clean. Cool in pan 10 minutes, and then transfer to cooling rack.

When cake is completely cool, top with powdered sugar or any of the frostings on pages 186–190.

Per slice: 361 calories, 19 g fat, 51 g carbohydrates, 4 g fiber, 4 g protein

Vanilla Cake

This cake is delicious with any of the frostings in this book, particularly one of the chocolate frostings on pages 186 and 187, and also tastes great served with all-fruit preserves and sliced fruit.

Makes one 8- or 9-inch cake (8 pieces)

¾	cup oat flour	1	cup granulated sugar
¾	cup gluten-free all-purpose flour	½	cup canola oil
1	tsp baking soda	½	cup rice milk
½	tsp salt	2	tsps vanilla
½	tsp xanthan gum	2	tbsps apple cider vinegar

Preheat oven to 375°F.

In a large bowl, whisk together both flours, baking soda, salt, xanthan gum, and sugar.

In a small bowl, combine canola oil, rice milk, and vanilla.

Add wet ingredients to dry. Stir apple cider vinegar into batter.

Pour batter into oiled cake pan.

Bake 30 to 35 minutes, or until a toothpick inserted into the center comes out clean.

VARIATION

You can add ½ cup of chocolate chips to the batter to turn this into a chocolate-chip cake.

Per serving: 298 calories, 15 fat, 40 g carbohydrates, 2 g fiber, 2 g protein

Desserts

Chocolate Frosting, Version One

If you top Chocolate Birthday Cake (page 184) or Vanilla Cake (page 185) with this scrumptious frosting, be prepared to lick the plate clean!

Makes about 1 cup (more than enough to frost a one-layer cake or 9 cupcakes)

2	tbsps nonhydrogenated palm oil shortening	Combine shortening, oil, vanilla, and 2 tablespoons rice milk in a food processor.
2	tbsps canola oil	In a separate bowl, combine powdered sugar and cocoa.
2	tbsps vanilla	
2–4	tbsps rice milk	Mix sugar and cocoa into wet ingredients until smooth.
2¼	cups powdered sugar	For thinner frosting, use a little more rice milk.
¼	cup cocoa	

Per serving, 9 servings: 188 calories, 6 g fat, 33 g carbohydrates, 1 g fiber, 1 g protein

Chocolate Frosting, Version Two

This frosting is a rich, ganache-style icing.

Makes more than enough to frost a one-layer cake or 9 cupcakes

¾ cup rice milk

2 cups chocolate chips

1 tsp vanilla

Heat rice milk until hot, but not boiling. Remove from heat; stir in chocolate chips and vanilla until smooth.

Refrigerate before using. Fluff cold frosting with a spoon or electric mixer before spreading on cake.

Per serving: 211 calories, 14 g fat, 26 g carbohydrates, 0 g fiber, 3 g protein

Vanilla Frosting

Although this frosting is delicious on cakes, it also transforms Autumn Pumpkin Muffins (page 144) or Double Chocolate Zucchini Muffins (page 151) into cupcakes.

Makes more than enough to frost one 8- or 9-inch cake or 9 cupcakes

2 tbsps nonhydrogenated palm oil shortening	Combine shortening, oil, vanilla, and rice milk in a bowl or food processor.
2 tbsps canola oil	Mix in powdered sugar until smooth.
1–2 tbsps vanilla extract, or to taste	For thinner frosting, use a little more rice milk.
2 tbsps rice milk	
2¼ cups powdered sugar	

Per serving: 183 calories, 6 g fat, 31 g carbohydrates, 0 g fiber, 0 g protein

Sunflower Seed Butter Frosting

For a really special dessert, frost Vanilla Cake (page 185) with this frosting and sprinkle chocolate chips between the layers and on top.

Makes more than enough frosting to frost a one-layer cake or 9 cupcakes

3 tbsps sunflower seed butter	Combine sunflower seed butter, vanilla, and rice milk in a food processor or bowl. Mix well.
2 tbsps vanilla	
2 tbsps rice milk	Add powdered sugar, one half at a time, mixing until smooth after each addition.
2¼ cups powdered sugar	

Per serving: 158 calories, 3 g fat, 32 g carbohydrates, 0 g fiber, 1 g protein

Coconut Frosting

This sweet and creamy frosting is a fantastic topping for Chocolate Birthday Cake (page 184), Double Chocolate Zucchini Muffins (page 151), or Carrot Cake Muffins (page 152).

Makes more than enough to frost one 8- or 9-inch cake or 9 cupcakes

3   tbsps coconut oil

3   tbsps coconut milk
     (light coconut milk
     is fine)

2¼ cups powdered sugar

Combine coconut oil and coconut milk in a food processor or bowl.

Add powdered sugar and blend until smooth.

Frosting will thicken as it sets, but you can add a little more powdered sugar if you want a thicker frosting.

Per serving, ⅑ of recipe: 161 calories, 5 g fat, 30 g carbohydrates, 0 g fiber, 0 g protein

Cinnamon Coffee Cake

The flour mixture in this cake makes for a lighter texture than using oat flour alone. However, if you want to throw together a quick snack for visitors and don't have potato starch, substitute oat flour and you will still have a really good coffee cake. Steel-cut oats add a nutty texture to this cake, but if you don't have them on hand, you can substitute old-fashioned rolled oats.

Makes 9 servings

1¾ cups gluten-free oat flour, divided

¼ cup potato starch

¾ tsp baking powder, divided

½ tsp baking soda

½ tsp salt

½ tsp xanthan gum

¼ cup applesauce

1 cup rice milk

1 tsp vanilla

½ cup canola oil, divided

¼ cup granulated sugar

½ cup packed light brown sugar

½ tsp cinnamon

¼ cup gluten-free steel-cut oats

Preheat oven to 350°F. Lightly oil a square baking pan.

In a medium bowl, using a whisk, combine 1½ cups of the oat flour, potato starch, ½ teaspoon baking powder, baking soda, salt, and xanthan gum.

In a large bowl, combine applesauce with ¼ teaspoon baking powder. To applesauce mixture, add rice milk, vanilla, ¼ cup canola oil, and granulated sugar.

Mix dry ingredients into wet.

continued

In a small bowl, combine brown sugar, the remaining ¼ cup oat flour, cinnamon, ¼ cup canola oil, and steel-cut oats.

Spread half the cake batter in baking pan. Top with half the brown sugar mixture. Spread remaining cake batter on top of that. Top with remaining brown sugar mixture.

Bake 45 minutes, or until golden brown and a toothpick inserted into the middle of the cake comes out clean.

Per serving: 248 calories, 15 g fat, 26 g carbohydrates, 2 g fiber, 4 g protein

Piecrust

A go-to pie crust comes in handy for a variety of dishes, both sweet and savory. If you're using the pie crust for a savory dish, like a vegetable tart, you can decrease or omit the agave nectar. If you don't need four piecrusts right away, freeze extra dough balls for future use.

Makes 4 crusts (8 slices each)

4	cups gluten-free oat flour
1	tbsp salt
1¾	cups soy-free vegetable shortening
¼	cup applesauce
¼	tsp baking powder
1	tbsp agave nectar
½	cup ice water

In a large bowl, combine flour and salt. Cut shortening into flour with a pastry blender or two knives.

In a small bowl, combine applesauce with baking powder. Add agave nectar and ice water to applesauce. Combine thoroughly.

Mix liquid ingredients into flour mixture.

Divide dough into four equal balls. Refrigerate for at least one hour.

Preheat oven to 375°F.

Flatten dough into a disk. Press dough into pie pan.

Bake for at least 15 minutes before filling.

Per slice: 145 calories, 12 g fat, 8 g carbohydrates, 1 g fiber, 2 g protein

Apple Pie

Not only will this pie fill your kitchen with a best-of-autumn aroma, but it will delight your taste buds with exceptional flavor! For a less sugary pie, use sweet apples, such as a blend of Golden Delicious and Pink Lady or Braeburn, and omit the turbinado sugar.

Makes 8 servings

2	*pie crusts*
6	*apples*
1	*tsp cinnamon*
¼	*tsp allspice*
½	*cup turbinado sugar*

Preheat oven to 375°F.

Prebake piecrusts. (If using recipe on page 193, prebake for 15 minutes, per directions.)

Peel, core, and slice apples. Toss apples with cinnamon, allspice, and sugar.

Fill one crust with apple mixture.

Top with second crust, press down on edges, and pierce the top crust.

Bake for 45 minutes.

TIP Choose apples that are full of flavor for the most flavorful pie. I like to mix Granny Smith with Jonathan or Macintosh.

Per serving: 400 calories, 24 g fat, 46 g carbohydrates, 5 g fiber, 3 g protein

Pumpkin Pie

This Thanksgiving holiday staple is creamy, spicy, and not too sweet. If the texture is too soft, refrigerate before serving.

Makes 9 servings

1	*piecrust*	*½*	*cup rice milk*
½	*cup applesauce*	*½*	*cup sugar*
½	*tsp baking powder*	*1*	*tsp cinnamon*
1	*15-ounce can pumpkin or scant 2 cups fresh pumpkin puree*	*½*	*tsp allspice*

Preheat oven to 375°F.

Prebake crust for 10 to 15 minutes.

In a large bowl, combine applesauce and baking powder. Mix in pumpkin, rice milk, sugar, cinnamon, and allspice. Blend thoroughly. Pour into piecrust.

Bake pie for 1 hour. Let pie cool completely on a cooling rack before serving.

TIP You can also make your own pumpkin puree. Slice a small pie pumpkin in half. Clean out the seeds, and use them for a different purpose. Set the pumpkin halves face down on a baking dish with a lip of at least ½ inch; fill with water. Bake in a preheated 350°F oven until the skin on the pumpkin starts to bubble (45 to 75 minutes). Check periodically to ensure that the water has not evaporated; add more if necessary. The skin should easily pull off. Then mash the pumpkin with a potato masher or puree in a food processor. One pumpkin should yield the scant two cups that you will need for this recipe.

Per serving: 201 calories, 11 g fat, 25 g carbohydrates, 2 g fiber, 2 g protein

Desserts

Chocolate-Dipped Strawberries

Keeping the leaves on the strawberries makes a very pretty presentation. I made these for my sister's baby shower, and they were a big hit.

20 servings

20 *large strawberries*

1 *cup allergen-free chocolate chips*

Wash strawberries, and let them completely dry.

In a small saucepan, heat chocolate chips over medium heat, stirring constantly until they are half melted. Remove from heat and continue to stir until completely melted.

Dip strawberries into melted chocolate. Place strawberries on wax-paper-lined baking sheets.

Refrigerate until ready to serve.

Per serving: 51 calories, 3 g fat, 7 g carbohydrates, 0 g fiber, 1 g protein

Hot Fudge Cake

This rich chocolate cake tastes as if it's been drenched in hot fudge. Serve it warm in bowls with Coconut Crème (page 198), sorbet, or sliced fruit. It's so good that guests frequently request it for holiday dessert.

Makes 9 servings

1¼ cups turbinado sugar, divided

1 cup gluten-free oat flour

½ cup cocoa, divided

2 tsps baking powder

¼ tsp salt

½ cup rice milk

⅓ cup canola oil

2 tsps vanilla

½ cup packed light brown sugar

1¼ cups hot water

Preheat oven to 350°F.

In a medium bowl, whisk together ¾ cup turbinado sugar, oat flour, ¼ cup cocoa, baking powder, and salt. Add rice milk, canola oil, and vanilla. Stir to combine. Scrape batter into an 8- or 9-inch-square cake pan.

In a small bowl, combine brown sugar, ½ cup turbinado sugar, and ¼ cup cocoa. Sprinkle over cake batter.

Gently pour hot water over cake batter.

Bake 35–40 minutes, until cake seems set and hot fudge is bubbling up between cake "islands."

Per slice: 275 calories, 10 g fat, 49 g carbohydrates, 2 g fiber, 2 g protein

Coconut Crème

When you need a cool, fresh, creamy topping for pie, cake, or sorbet, this easy crème is hard to beat.

Makes 12 servings

Place an unopened can of coconut milk in the refrigerator for at least 3 hours or overnight. The coconut milk will separate into crème and water. Open can; pour off the water, using the top of the can to hold the crème in the can.

Spoon thickened coconut milk into a bowl. Use the crème in place of whipped topping anytime a cool, creamy addition is desired.

Per 2 tbsp serving: 56 calories, 6 g fat, 1 g carbohydrates, 0 g fiber, 1 g protein

Apple Crisp

Steel-cut oats add a nutty texture to this crisp. If you don't have steel-cut oats, add an additional ¼ cup of oat flour. Serve this apple crisp warm with a scoop of sorbet or granita. (I like lemon or coconut.)

Makes 6 servings

6	medium-sized apples
¾	cup packed light brown sugar
1	tsp vanilla
½	cup oat flour
¼	cup steel cut oats
¼	cup canola oil
	canola oil spray

Preheat oven to 400°F.

Peel, core, and thinly slice apples.

In a small bowl, combine sugar, vanilla, oat flour, oats, and oil.

Spray a 2-quart casserole with canola oil. Spread apple slices in bottom of casserole and top with sugar mixture.

Bake 40 minutes.

Per serving: 322 calories, 10 g fat, 59 g carbohydrates, 5 g fiber, 2 g protein

Desserts

Strawberry Shortcake

If you like a sweeter shortcake, double the amount of turbinado sugar.

Makes 4 servings

2	cups thinly sliced strawberries	2	tbsps all-vegetable shortening
¼	cup granulated sugar	½	cup rice milk
¾	cups gluten-free all-purpose flour	½	tsp lemon juice
½	tsp baking powder	½	tsp vanilla
¼	tsp baking soda	1	tsp turbinado sugar
⅛	tsp salt	½	cup Coconut Crème (page 198)
¼	tsp xanthan gum		

Toss strawberries with granulated sugar. Refrigerate strawberries for an hour. Preheat oven to 425°F.

In a large bowl, combine flour, baking powder, baking soda, salt, and xanthan gum using a whisk. Cut shortening into flour mixture using a pastry cutter or two knives.

In a small bowl, combine rice milk and lemon juice. Add vanilla to rice milk mixture.

Add liquid to flour mixture; stir to combine.

Drop heaping tablespoons of batter onto ungreased cookie sheets. Sprinkle biscuits with turbinado sugar.

Bake 12–15 minutes, or until golden.

To assemble shortcakes, slice biscuits in half. Pour ¼ of the strawberries onto the bottom halves; replace top halves. Add a drizzle of the strawberry liquid and ¼ of the coconut crème.

Per serving: 298 calories, 14 g fat, 43 g carbohydrates, 4 g fiber, 4 g protein

Blueberry Crumble Cake

This not-too-sweet coffee cake has a crust that tastes like graham crackers. It's delicious, but messy, so make sure to eat with a fork!

Makes 9 servings

1½ cups gluten-free oat flour

¼ cup potato starch

1 tsp salt

¼ tsp xanthan gum

1 tsp baking soda

½ cup applesauce

½ tsp baking powder

1 tsp vanilla

¾ cup canola oil, divided

2 cups fresh or frozen blueberries

2 tsps plus ½ cup sugar, divided

½ cup rolled oats

Preheat oven to 350°F. Oil an 8-inch square pan.

In a medium bowl, combine oat flour, potato starch, salt, xanthan gum, and baking soda.

In a separate bowl, combine applesauce with baking powder. Add vanilla and ½ cup canola oil. Mix dry mixture into wet mixture.

Spread mixture into oiled pan. Bake 20 minutes.

In a small bowl, combine blueberries with 2 teaspoons sugar.

In a separate bowl, combine ½ cup sugar, oats, and ¼ cup canola oil.

Raise oven temperature to 400°F.

Spread blueberries over cake. Spread oat mixture over blueberries.

Bake 35–40 minutes, or until the topping is lightly golden. Cool completely before cutting into bars.

Per serving: 371 calories, 20 g fat, 47 g carbohydrates, 2 g fiber, 3 g protein

Caramel Brownie Sundaes

The caramel sauce in this sundae is actually mixed into the soft brownie layer.

Makes 9 servings

¾	cup granulated sugar	½	tsp salt
½	cup canola oil	½	cup applesauce
2	tbsps water	½	tsp baking powder
1	cup allergy-free chocolate chips	1	cup Caramel Sauce (page 203)
1½	tsps vanilla		canola oil for pan
1¼	cups gluten-free oat flour	4½	cups coconut sorbet
½	tsp baking soda		

Preheat oven to 350°F. Oil an 8- or 9-inch square pan.

Combine sugar, oil, and water in a microwave-safe bowl or small saucepan. If using a microwave, heat on high for 1 minute. If using a saucepan, heat over medium heat, stirring until hot, but not boiling (about 2 minutes). Stir the chocolate chips and the vanilla into the sugar mixture, until the chocolate is melted. Set aside.

In a separate bowl, combine the flour, baking soda, and salt. Set aside.

In a small bowl, combine applesauce with baking powder. Add applesauce mixture to chocolate. Stir to combine. Add the flour mixture to the chocolate mixture, one half at a time.

Pour the batter into the prepared pan. Spread Caramel Sauce over the top of the brownie batter. Using a knife, mix caramel sauce into batter.

Bake 45 minutes. Remove cake from oven. Set aside to cool somewhat. Scoop warm brownie into a bowl and top with a scoop of sorbet.

Per serving: 597 calories, 28 g fat, 88 g carbohydrates, 1 g fiber, 3 g protein

Caramel Sauce

Craving caramel apples? Enjoy this fall treat by dipping apple slices in this super-delicious dipping sauce. It also makes a great topping for sorbet, coconut-based ice cream, pies, or whatever else you can think of. The caramel sky's the limit!

Makes 2 cups

¾ cup coconut milk, divided

2 tbsps kuzu root starch

½ cup coconut oil

2 cups packed light brown sugar

In a small bowl, combine ¼ cup coconut milk with kuzu root (or cornstarch). Stir until kuzu root (or cornstarch) is dissolved.

In a small saucepan, melt coconut oil over medium heat. Add brown sugar; stir to combine. Add remaining coconut milk and bring to a boil. Boil 3–4 minutes.

Remove from heat and stir in kuzu root (or cornstarch) mixture.

Caramel sauce is pretty thin when it's warm, but will thicken up when cooled.

TIP Kuzu root is a thickener found in Asian markets or the Asian aisle of well-stocked grocery stores. You can substitute cornstarch if you don't have kuzu root.

Per 2 tbsp serving: 188 calories, 9 g fat, 28 g carbohydrates, 0 g fiber, 0 g protein

Desserts

Decadent Chocolate Brownies

It's a breeze to cut these soft, extra-rich brownies if you refrigerate them first.

Makes 12 brownies

¾ cup sugar

½ cup canola oil

2 tbsps water

2 cups chocolate chips, divided

1½ tsps vanilla

1¼ cups oat flour

½ tsp baking soda

½ tsp salt

½ cup applesauce

½ tsp baking powder

canola oil in a pump spray can

Preheat oven to 350°F. Spray an 8- or 9-inch square pan.

Combine sugar, oil, and water in a microwave-safe bowl or small saucepan. If using a microwave, heat on high for 1 minute. If using a saucepan, heat over medium heat, stirring until hot, but not boiling (about 2 minutes). Stir half the chocolate chips and the vanilla into the sugar mixture until the chips are melted. Set aside.

In a separate bowl, combine the flour, baking soda, and salt. Set aside.

Combine applesauce and baking powder. Add the applesauce mixture to the chocolate. Stir to combine.

Add the flour mixture, one half at a time. Add the remaining chocolate chips. Spread in prepared pan.

Bake 30–35 minutes. Cool completely before cutting.

Per serving: 323 calories, 20 g fat, 38 g carbohydrates, 1 g fiber, 3 g protein

Chocolate Chip Cookies

These cookies are delicious, but can be a little fragile. Make sure to cool them completely before serving. Store extra cookies (if there are any left!) in the freezer; this will make them sturdier.

Makes about 48 cookies

3	cups gluten-free oat flour
1	tsp baking soda
½	tsp salt
½	cup applesauce
½	tsp baking powder
¾	cup canola oil
1½	cups packed dark brown sugar
1	tbsp vanilla
2	cups chocolate chips

Preheat oven to 375°F.

Combine flour, baking soda, and salt in a medium bowl. Set aside.

In a large bowl, combine applesauce and baking powder. Add oil, brown sugar, and vanilla to applesauce mixture.

Add dry ingredients to wet one half at a time. Stir just to combine. Stir in chocolate chips.

Drop batter by the tablespoon onto ungreased cookie sheets (or cookie sheets covered with parchment paper).

Bake 10–12 minutes. Let cool on cookie sheets for about 3 minutes before moving to a cooling rack to cool completely.

Per cookie: 118 calories, 6 g fat, 15 g carbohydrates, 0 g fiber, 1 g protein

Desserts

Chocolate Cookies

You can turn these cookies into an upscale sandwich cookie by putting two cookies together with any delicious Welcoming Kitchen frosting. Coconut Frosting (page 190) is particularly good!

Makes 42 cookies

3	cups oat flour	½	tsp baking powder
1	tsp baking soda	½	cup canola oil
½	tsp salt	2	tbsps blackstrap molasses
1	cup allergy-free chocolate chips	1	cup light brown sugar
½	cup applesauce	1	tbsp vanilla

Preheat oven to 375°F.

In a medium bowl, combine flour, baking soda, and salt with a whisk.

Either in a small saucepan on the stove or using a microwave, melt chocolate chips.

In a large bowl, combine applesauce and baking powder. Add canola oil, molasses, brown sugar, and vanilla to the applesauce mixture. Scrape melted chocolate chips into wet ingredients. Stir to combine. Thoroughly mix dry ingredients into wet.

Drop generous teaspoonfuls of batter onto ungreased cookie sheets (or cookie sheets lined with parchment paper). Bake 10–12 minutes. Transfer to cooling racks; cool completely.

OAT-FREE VARIATION

Replace oat flour with 3 cups gluten-free all-purpose flour and ½ teaspoon xanthan gum.

Per cookie: 95 calories, 5 g fat, 13 g carbohydrates, 0 g fiber, 1 g protein

Oatmeal Raisin Cookies

These cookies are our family and friends' new favorites. Store them in the freezer if there are any left after a day or two.

Makes 48 cookies

1 cup gluten-free oat flour

2 cups gluten-free rolled oats (old-fashioned oatmeal)

½ tsp cinnamon

½ tsp baking soda

½ tsp salt

¼ cup applesauce

¼ tsp baking powder

½ cup brown sugar

¼ cup maple syrup

½ cup canola oil

½ cup raisins

½ cup allergy-free chocolate chips (optional)

2 tbsps kuzu root or cornstarch

Preheat oven to 350°F.

In a medium bowl, combine oat flour, rolled oats, cinnamon, baking soda, and salt with a whisk. Set aside.

In a large bowl, combine applesauce with baking powder. Add brown sugar, syrup, and oil to the applesauce mixture.

Slowly add dry ingredients to wet. Stir in raisins (and chocolate chips, if using).

Drop batter by teaspoons onto ungreased cookie sheets.

Bake 13–15 minutes or until golden brown. Let cool for 3–5 minutes on cookie sheet before removing to cooling racks. Let cool completely.

Per cookie: 69 calories, 3 g fat, 10 g carbohydrates, 1 g fiber, 1 g protein

Rolling Pin Sugar Cookies

Get your cookie cutters out! With this recipe you can make really great decorating-ready cookies that will be safe for every snacker. (Soy-free Earth Balance was the only nonhydrogenated butter substitute that fits the Welcoming Kitchen model that I could find at the time of writing this book; remember to check the ingredients every time, though, as formulations can change.)

Makes 36 cookies

1 cup soy-free Earth Balance nonhydrogenated butter substitute

1 cup sugar

½ cup applesauce

2½ tsps baking powder, divided

1 tsp vanilla

4 cups gluten-free all-purpose flour

½ tsp xanthan gum

½ tsp salt

¼ cup plain coconut milk-based yogurt

powdered sugar for dusting work surface

Put a cookie sheet into the refrigerator or freezer to chill.

Cream butter substitute and sugar together.

In a separate bowl, combine applesauce with ½ teaspoon baking powder. Add applesauce and vanilla to creamed mixture; blend together.

In a medium bowl, combine flour, xanthan gum, 2 teaspoons baking powder, and salt. Whisk together.

Slowly mix flour mixture into wet ingredients.

Mix yogurt into batter.

Shape dough into a disk; wrap in plastic wrap or seal in a zip-top bag. Refrigerate for at least an hour.

Preheat oven to 350°F.

Dust work surface and rolling pin with powdered sugar. Roll dough ¼-inch thick. Re-chill dough by placing a cold cookie sheet on top. Cut with cookie cutters.

Bake on ungreased cookie sheets or on cookie sheets lined with parchment paper for 13–15 minutes or until golden.

OAT FLOUR VARIATION

Substitute 4 cups gluten-free oat flour for the gluten-free all-purpose flour and xanthan gum.

Per cookie: 75 calories, 5 g fat, 8 g carbohydrates, 1 g fiber, 0 g protein

Crispy Sunflower Seed Butter Treats

Looking for a not-too-sweet crunchy treat? Look no further—this is the one for you!

Makes 21 treats

½ cup sunflower seed butter

¼ cup agave nectar

½ cup oat flour

1 cup crispy rice cereal

Preheat oven to 350°F.

In a large bowl, combine sunflower seed butter and agave nectar.

Thoroughly mix in oat flour. Stir in crispy rice cereal.

Form dough into balls about 1 inch in diameter. Place on ungreased cookie sheets.

Bake 8 minutes. Cool on cooling racks.

CRISPY COCOA TREAT VARIATION

Add ¼ cup cocoa to sunflower seed butter and agave nectar mixture.

Per serving: 62 calories, 3 g fat, 8 g carbohydrates, 1 g fiber, 2 g protein

Cinnamon Chocolate Chip Cookies

For people who don't like chocolate, you can skip the chocolate chips and enjoy a delicious cinnamon cookie instead.

Makes 36 cookies

2	cups gluten-free all-purpose flour	
½	tsp xanthan gum	
1	tsp cinnamon	
1	tsp salt	
1	tsp baking soda	
½	cup applesauce	
½	tsp baking powder	
1	cup turbinado sugar	
½	cup canola oil	
¼	cup brewed coffee (decaf is fine)	
1	cup chocolate chips	

In a medium bowl, combine flour, xanthan gum, cinnamon, salt, and baking soda.

In a large bowl, combine applesauce with baking powder. Mix turbinado sugar, oil, and coffee into applesauce mixture.

Add dry ingredients to wet. Stir chocolate chips into batter.

Refrigerate batter for at least an hour before baking.

Preheat oven to 350°F.

Drop dough by tablespoons onto ungreased baking sheets. Bake 12–15 minutes. Let cool on cooling racks.

Per cookie: 97 calories, 5 fat, 14 g carbohydrates, 1 g fiber, 1 g protein

Desserts

Sunflower Seed Butter Cookies

Oat-free cookies are perfect for people who aren't huge chocoholics—or for anyone who really loves a scrumptious cookie! If you are baking these buttery cookies in batches, keep the dough for the later batches in the refrigerator so it doesn't get too soft to handle.

Makes about 48 cookies

1⅔	cups gluten-free all purpose flour
1	tsp xanthan gum
½	tsp baking powder
½	tsp baking soda
¼	tsp salt
1	cup sunflower seed butter
¼	cup canola oil
⅔	cup packed brown sugar
½	cup granulated sugar
½	cup applesauce plus ½ tsp baking powder

Preheat oven to 375°F.

In a medium bowl, combine flour, xanthan gum, baking powder, baking soda, and salt. Set aside.

In a large bowl, mix together remaining ingredients until smooth.

Add dry ingredients to wet, one half at a time.

Form the dough into 1½ inch balls. Place on ungreased cookie sheets. Press the tines of a fork into each ball, forming a criss-cross pattern.

Bake 12–15 minutes. Remove to cooling rack to cool.

Per serving: 73 calories, 4 g fat, 10 g carbohydrates, 0 g fiber, 1 g protein

CHOCOLATE FLOWER VARIATION

This delightful cookie looks like a flower with a dark center and light petals.

Makes about 48 cookies

1   batch Sunflower Seed
    Butter Cookies dough
    (page 212)

1 cup chocolate chips

Preheat oven to 375°F.

Form the dough into 1½ inch balls. Place on ungreased cookie sheets. Flatten each ball with the back of a teaspoon, making a small crater in the center of each. Fill each center with chocolate chips.

Bake 12–15 minutes.

Swirl the warm chocolate with the back of a spoon if you don't want individual chips in the center of the "flower."

Desserts

Chocolate Pudding

Warm pudding is a delight in cold weather, but when the temperature outside is on the rise, you can pour this delicious chocolate pudding into ice-pop molds and make frozen pudding pops!

Makes 3 servings

¼ cup cocoa

¼ cup sugar

2 tsps vanilla

   hot water

2 tbsps kuzu root starch
   (or cornstarch)

¼ cup cold water

2 cups rice milk

In a small bowl, mix cocoa, sugar, and vanilla. Add hot water, one tablespoon at a time, until dissolved into a thick paste.

In a separate small bowl, mix kuzu and cold water until dissolved.

Heat rice milk in a small saucepan. Add cocoa mixture and kuzu mixture. Bring to a boil. Stir constantly until thick.

Pour into bowls. Chill until ready to serve.

Per serving: 135 calories, 2 g fat, 25 g carbohydrates, 1 g fiber, 2 g protein

Chocolate Rice Pudding

This is a creamy, homey, delicious treat. For a totally decadent experience, serve it warm with coconut sorbet. I suggest putting a cookie sheet on the rack beneath the pudding because some liquid may escape while it's baking.

Makes 6 servings

3	cups rice milk
1	cup brewed coffee
⅔	cup turbinado sugar
1	tbsp vanilla
½	tsp cinnamon
¼	tsp salt
1	cup rinsed arborio rice
⅔	cup allergy-free chocolate chips

Preheat oven to 325°F.

In a medium saucepan, combine rice milk, coffee, sugar, vanilla, cinnamon, and salt. Bring to a boil.

Combine rice and chocolate chips in a 2-quart casserole. Add milk mixture; stir to combine.

Cover and bake for 1 hour.

Per serving: 374 calories, 9 g fat, 72 g carbohydrates, 1 g fiber, 4 g protein

Coconut Rice Pudding

This is the ultimate comfort food. It's creamy and sweet, with a subtle coconut flavor. Best of all, it's super-easy to put together any time with ingredients you can always have on hand in your pantry. If you want to reduce the fat content in this dish, substitute light coconut milk for regular.

Makes 8 servings

4   cups coconut milk (either light or regular)

⅔   cup granulated sugar

1   tbsp vanilla

¼   tsp salt

1   cup arborio rice, rinsed

Preheat oven to 325°F.

In a medium saucepan, combine coconut milk, sugar, vanilla, and salt. Bring to a boil.

In a casserole, combine hot liquid and rice. Stir to combine. Cover casserole and bake for one hour.

Stir before serving.

Per serving: 378 calories, 24 g fat, 39 g carbohydrates, 1 g fiber, 2 g protein

Raspberry Honeydew Sorbet

For a seedless sorbet, puree the raspberries separately and then press the puree through a fine-mesh strainer. Add the seedless puree to honeydew and apple juice and then proceed with the recipe.

Makes 4 cups

½   medium honeydew
1½ cups raspberries
½   cup apple juice

In a food processor or blender, puree all ingredients together. Pour into a freezer-safe container, such as a covered Pyrex container. Place in freezer.

After 1½–2 hours, fluff sorbet with a fork; then return to freezer.

After 2 more hours, fluff sorbet with a fork and return to freezer. Continue this process every couple of hours until ready to serve.

If you freeze the sorbet overnight, set it out on the counter a few minutes before you begin the fluffing process.

TIP If you have an ice cream maker, chill the puree for several hours in the refrigerator, then follow the instructions for making ice cream with your machine.

Per cup: 75 calories, 0 g fat, 18 g carbohydrates, 4 g fiber, 1 g protein

Coconut Sorbet

Make this sorbet the day you want to serve it, if possible. The more often you refreeze it, the larger the ice crystals will be, and your sorbet will be more icy than creamy.

Makes 6 servings

1   6-ounce container
     vanilla-flavored
     coconut-based yogurt

1   13.5-ounce can
     coconut milk (either
     light or regular)

2   tbsps granulated
     sugar

Combine all ingredients in a blender. Blend until smooth.

Pour into a freezer-safe container. Place in freezer. After 1½ hours, fluff mixture with a fork.

Continue fluffing every hour or so until ready to serve.

TIP If you have an ice cream maker, chill the puree for several hours in the refrigerator, then follow the instructions for making ice cream with your machine.

Per serving: 161 calories, 15 g fat, 8 g carbohydrates, 1 g fiber, 1 g protein

Sorbet Sandwiches

These "ice cream" sandwiches are a summertime sensation! The consistency of commercially prepared sorbet works slightly better than homemade sorbet in these treats, but you can use whatever sorbet you happen to have.

Makes 6 sandwiches

12 Chocolate Chip Cookies (page 205)

2   cups sorbet (strawberry or coconut work really nicely)

Divide and spread sorbet on top of six cookies. Top with remaining cookies.

Wrap sandwiches individually in plastic wrap and then aluminum foil.

Freeze until ready to serve.

Per serving: 251 calories, 10 g fat, 39 g carbohydrates, 1 g fiber, 2 g protein

Blueberry Coconut Ice

This recipe is a great jumping-off place for experimenting with different flavors—like strawberries with strawberry preserves or pineapple with orange marmalade. Any of these combos is sure to please, and what could be more refreshing on a hot summer day?

Makes 2 ½ cups

2   *cups frozen blueberries*

½   *cup all-fruit blueberry preserves*

½   *cup agave nectar*

1   *cup coconut milk*

Thoroughly blend all ingredients in a food processor. Scoop mixture into a flat-bottomed baking dish, cover, and freeze.

After one hour, fluff ice with a fork and return to the freezer. Continue fluffing with fork and freezing every 45 minutes or so until ice is frozen enough to scoop and eat with a spoon.

For storage, place a piece of waxed paper or plastic wrap on the surface of the ice before sealing in an air-tight, freezer-safe container. If the ice is too hard before serving, let it soften on the counter for a few minutes.

TIP If you have an ice cream maker, chill the puree for several hours in the refrigerator, then follow the instructions for making ice cream with your machine.

Per ½ cup serving: 306 calories, 10 g fat, 56 g carbohydrates, 4 g fiber, 1 g protein

Fruit Smoothie Ice Pops

Who needs popsicles full of sugar and food coloring when nutritious and delicious ice pops are this easy? Use the Good Morning Smoothie recipe (page 173) to make these refreshing treats.

1   recipe for fruit
     smoothies (page 173)

Fill an ice pop mold or ice-cube tray with the smoothie mixture. Cover with plastic wrap, and insert toothpicks into the center of each cube. Place in freezer.

Once the mixture's frozen, carefully remove the plastic wrap and briefly run the bottom of the ice-cube tray under warm water to loosen the mini-pops.

Per 1 ice-cube-size serving: 15 calories, 0 g fat, 3 g carbohydrates, 0 g fiber, 0 g protein

Strawberry Chocolate Chip Frozen Yogurt Pops

If you want to make this fruity and chocolate-y yogurt pop even sweeter, add more agave nectar.

Makes 7 pops

2	6-ounce containers plain coconut-based yogurt
6	sliced strawberries
¼	cup chocolate chips
2	tbsps agave nectar
¼	cup strawberry all-fruit preserves

Combine all ingredients in a blender. Mix completely.

Pour into an ice-pop mold. Freeze until solid (about 3 hours).

Per serving: 111 calories, 4 g fat, 18 g carbohydrates, 2 g fiber, 1 g protein

Hot Chocolate

Hot chocolate paired with a slice of Zucchini Bread (page 158) makes a great post-snow warm-you-up!

Makes 1 serving

1	tbsp sugar	In an empty coffee cup, combine sugar and cocoa.
2	tsps cocoa	
½	tsp vanilla	Add vanilla and stir to make a paste.
1	cup rice milk	In a small saucepan, heat rice milk until hot, but not boiling.
		Add rice milk to cocoa mixture. Stir thoroughly.

Per serving: 180 calories, 3 g fat, 37 g carbohydrates, 1 g fiber, 2 g protein

CHOCOLATE CANDIES

Allergen-free chocolate chips allow kids of all ages to enjoy a candy-bar treat. Make and serve these candies in a muffin paper because they get messy when they start to melt. Store candies in the refrigerator. They will keep their texture for well over an hour at room temperature (unless the room is very warm).

Chocolate-Raisin Clusters

Makes 12 large candies or 24 small candies

1 cup allergen-free chocolate chips

1 cup raisins

Line a standard muffin pan or mini muffin pan with muffin papers.

Heat chocolate chips over medium-low flame, stirring constantly until almost completely melted. Remove from heat and continue stirring until chocolate is completely melted. Stir raisins into melted chocolate.

Use a tablespoon to fill large muffin papers or a teaspoon to fill small muffin papers.

Refrigerate candies for at least 1½ hours.

Per large candy: 116 calories, 4 g fat, 19 g carbohydrates, 1 g fiber, 1 g protein

Chocolate-Covered Crispy Rice

Makes 12 large candies or 24 small candies

1   cup allergen-free
    chocolate chips

1   cup gluten-free
    crisp rice cereal

Line a standard muffin pan or mini muffin pan with muffin papers.

Heat chocolate chips over medium-low flame, stirring constantly until almost completely melted. Remove from heat and continue stirring until chocolate is completely melted.

Stir cereal into melted chocolate.

Use a tablespoon to fill large muffin papers or a teaspoon to fill small muffin papers. Smooth candy to fill paper.

Refrigerate candies for at least 1½ hours.

Per large candy: 84 calories, 4 g fat, 10 g carbohydrates, 0 g fiber, 1 g protein

Chocolate–Sunflower Seed Butter Cups

Makes 24

1   cup crispy rice cereal

½   cup sunflower seed
    butter

2   cups allergen-free
    chocolate chips

Line a mini muffin pan with paper liners.

In a food processor, combine rice cereal and sunflower seed butter. Blend together until cereal is completely crushed.

In a small saucepan, heat chocolate chips over medium heat, stirring until chocolate is halfway melted. Remove from heat and continue stirring until completely melted.

Spread 1½ teaspoons melted chocolate into each muffin paper. Top chocolate with 1 teaspoon sunflower seed butter mixture. Top each candy with 1½ teaspoons melted chocolate.

Refrigerate for at least one hour before serving.

Keep candies in the refrigerator before serving, as the chocolate will begin to melt in a warm room.

Per serving: 110 calories, 8 g fat, 11 g carbohydrates, 0 g fiber, 2 g protein

Chocolate Peppermint Cups

These are the ultimate holiday candies. You can make an extra-large batch and give some away for gifts. They look especially festive if you can find shiny candy wrappers. My boys love smashing up the candy canes, so it's a great holiday activity that we can do together.

Makes 18 candies

4–5 *standard-size allergen-free,*
   gluten-free candy canes

¼ *cup rice milk*

2½ *cups allergen-free, gluten-free*
   chocolate chips

Line a mini muffin pan with mini muffin papers.

Crush candy canes in their wrappers by smashing them with a rolling pin, or cover unwrapped candy canes with a towel and smash them through the towel. Four or 5 candy canes will make about 5 tablespoons of crumbs.

In a small saucepan, heat rice milk until it is just about to boil. Turn off heat. Stir 1 cup chocolate chips into rice milk; continue stirring until chocolate is completely melted. Stir crushed candy canes into melted chocolate. Set aside.

In another small saucepan, heat remaining chocolate chips, stirring constantly until about halfway melted. Remove from heat, and continue to stir until completely melted.

Spoon about ½ teaspoon of the melted chocolate into a muffin paper. Top with about 1 teaspoon of the peppermint chocolate. Cover the peppermint chocolate with another ½ teaspoon of melted chocolate.

Continue with remaining papers, one at a time. Cover muffin pan with waxed paper and refrigerate for at least one hour.

Per serving: 134 calories, 7 g fat, 16 g carbohydrates, 1 g fiber, 2 g protein

Desserts

SPECIAL MENUS
from a
Welcoming Kitchen

....

Every year we have a big, casual dinner party for the holidays with lots of appetizers, chili and rice, and a table full of cookies, mini cupcakes, and candies. I can't think of anything that makes the holidays more festive for me than feeding a huge crowd delicious food that is safe for every single one of my guests. I hope that you have as much fun putting together meals for your loved ones as I do!

Weekend Brunch

Brunch Hash

Fruit Kabobs

Biscuits with Assorted Jams

Apple Crisp

Holiday Dinner

Olivada Crostini

Artichoke-Portabella Risotto

Italian Eggplant

Green Salad with Fresh Strawberries and Red Wine and Lemon Vinaigrette

Hot Fudge Cake with Coconut Crème and/or Apple Pie

Game Day Buffet

Chipotle Guacamole

Lime-Lover's Salsa

Tortilla Chips and
Raw Vegetables

Chili

Chili Toppings:
*Diced Red Onions, Diced Tomatoes,
Chopped Avocado, Crumbled Corn
Chips or Tortilla Chips*

Country Corn Muffins

Green Salad with
Lemon Dill Salad Dressing

Oatmeal Raisin Cookies

Decadent Chocolate Brownies

Sunflower Seed Butter Cookies

Dinner al Fresco

Jerk Portabella Mushroom

Baked Beans

Ruby Coleslaw

Summertime Corn Salad

Oat-Cornmeal Bread

Strawberry Shortcake

Soup Buffet

Split Pea Soup

Kitchen Sink Soup

Two-Potato Soup

Sweet Potato Biscuits

Country Corn Muffins

Beer Bread

Chocolate Birthday Cake
with Coconut Frosting

Cocktail Party

Artichoke Fritters

Pesto-Stuffed Cherry Tomatoes

Polenta and Herb-Stuffed
Mushrooms

Crostini with Assorted Toppings

Sesame-Free Hummus
with Raw Vegetables

Laura's Layered Taco Dip with
Baked Tortilla Chips

RESOURCES

....

Many helpful resources are available for individuals and families that live with food allergies or other food-sensitivity issues. Your local hospital can provide a wealth of information, as can the organizations listed below:

Food Allergy and
Anaphylaxis Network
www.foodallergy.org

Food Allergy Initiative
www.faiusa.org

ELL Foundation
www.ellfoundation.org

Allergy Sense
www.allergysense.com

Mallergies
www.mallergies.com

Celiac Sprue Association
www.csaceliacs.org

Celiac.com
www.celiac.com

Centers for Disease
Control, Autism
Information Center
www.cdc.gov/ncbddd/autism

Autism Speaks
www.autismspeaks.org

Welcoming Kitchen blog
www.welcomingkitchen.com

ABOUT THE AUTHORS

Kim Lutz is a home cook and mother of two. She is the co-author with Megan Hart of *The Everything Organic Cooking for Baby & Toddler Book*, *The Everything Guide to Cooking for Children with Autism*, and the blog **welcomingkitchen.com**. Kim lives in Chicago with her two sons and husband.

Megan Hart, MS, RD, is a registered dietitian who specializes in pediatric nutrition. She currently works as a senior clinical dietitian at Children's Memorial Hospital in Chicago. Megan lives in Chicago with her husband and son.

Photograph of Kim Lutz by Sandra Wettig · Photograph of Megan Hart by Andrew Hart

LIQUID

This chart can also be used for small amounts of
dry ingredients, such as salt and baking powder.

U.S. quantity	Metric equivalent
¼ teaspoon	1 ml
½ teaspoon	2.5 ml
¾ teaspoon	4 ml
1 teaspoon	5 ml
1¼ teaspoons	6 ml
1½ teaspoons	7.5 ml
1¾ teaspoons	8.5 ml
2 teaspoons	10 ml
1 tablespoon	15 ml
2 tablespoons	30 ml
⅛ cup	30 ml
¼ cup *(2 fluid ounces)*	60 ml
⅓ cup	80 ml
½ cup *(4 fluid ounces)*	120 ml
⅔ cup	160 ml
¾ cup *(6 fluid ounces)*	180 ml
1 cup *(8 fluid ounces)*	240 ml
1½ cups *(12 fluid ounces)*	350 ml
3 cups	700 ml
4 cups *(1 quart)*	950 ml *(.95 liter)*

DRY

Ingredient	1 cup	¾ cup	⅔ cup	½ cup	⅓ cup	¼ cup	2 tbsp
All-purpose gluten-free flour	160g	120g	106g	80g	53g	40g	20g
Granulated sugar	200g	150g	130g	100g	65g	50g	25g
Confectioners' sugar	100g	75g	70g	50g	35g	25g	13g
Brown sugar, firmly packed	180g	135g	120g	90g	60g	45g	23g
Cornmeal	160g	120g	100g	80g	50g	40g	20g
Cornstarch	120g	90g	80g	60g	40g	30g	15g
Shortening	190g	140g	125g	95g	65g	48g	24g
Chopped fruits and vegetables	150g	110g	100g	75g	50g	40g	20g
Chopped seeds	150g	110g	100g	75g	50g	40g	20g
Ground seeds	120g	90g	80g	60g	40g	30g	15g

INDEX

••••••••••••••••••••••